Bringing Music to Life

G-7413

Bringing Music to Life

Barry Green

Author of
The Inner Game of Music
and *The Mastery of Music*

With a Foreword by
Don Campbell
Author of *The Mozart Effect* ®

GIA Publications, Inc.
Chicago

Bringing Music to Life
Barry Green

GIA Publications, Inc.
7404 S Mason Ave
Chicago IL 60638
www.giamusic.com/

G-7413
ISBN: 978-1-57999-757-1

Table of Contents

PART II: The Three Techniques

PART III: Inspiration

Foreword
Don Campbell

This is not a book to read, it is a book to live. If you are a musician, it can help you reformat your creativity. If you are not a musician, it can help you take those first rhythmic steps to joy and expression. If you have lost your confidence in performance, *Bringing Music to Life* can launch your courage, vision, and vitality.

Barry Green has lived on the edge. I remember watching him perform with the Cincinnati Symphony Orchestra nearly thirty years ago. With his double bass as a steady date, he stood on the edge of the stage. At the College-Conservatory of Music, his "Green Machine" concerts brought the audience to the edge of their seats as pots and pans accompanied the artists onstage. His appetite to keep music fresh, alive and creative has heralded professionals, youngsters and students all over the world to not fall into the doldrums of inhibition, nervousness or fear of the sonic unknown.

This book is like a series of bulletin boards filled with memories, exercises, stories and suggestions. It just can't be read. You have to trust Barry and just open this book like some kind of intuitive oracle and try a page or two at a time. From your pulse to your expression and movement, he will challenge your left brain to let go and follow the dance of music.

So often music teachers and students fall into the abyss of technique and method. Unlike painting, sculpture, and poetry, music often relies on the skill of composers who are telling us what to do. How many graduates of music schools live in the expression of the great masters rather than their own hearts? We can make a career in the pre-existing literature and repertoire of composers, but when we touch our own hearts both old and new music come alive.

What calls us to music is not just to "reproduce" what others have written. It is what is beyond "paper music" that is essential no matter how much we have developed our talent. What calls us is to be in union with the rhythm and pulse of life so we become more alive with every note…and to share that vitality with others.

Music is a living moment that passes through time with sound. From the ecstasy to agony in performance, we can quicken the experience by putting our mind and body in gear for expression with the many suggestions in this book.

What Barry, David Darling and many musicians proclaim is the power of music is for everyone. With children and elders, there is an immediate alignment with the rhythm of a drumbeat. The sound of singing voice calls us to listen and modify our attention to the world around us.

There is no need to read this book cover to cover in sequential order from chapter 1 to 9. Read it from here to there, in parts, sections or in a quiet flow. Just uncover your intuition and let the music do its magic. Whether you are just a listener, a dancer, a performer or a student, the time is always ready to turn the now into music.

—Don Campbell
Boulder, Colorado

Don Campbell is the author of twenty-two books,
including The Mozart Effect®.

Introduction
Jam—Scat—Move—Groove

Get lively! Bring your music to life! Jam—Scat—Move—Groove!

That's what this book is about—pouring yourself, body and soul, into your music making so that the music you make truly comes alive!

And while I'll be talking mainly about music making, the same goes for other performing artists, too.

Performer, Performance and Audience

As a performer, you have a message to communicate to others, and you naturally want to communicate it as richly and vibrantly as possible. Perhaps you're bringing to life some great work by Mozart or Brahms. It's a privilege to act as the messenger of some of the greatest words, images or music the great masters of artistic history have ever produced. Or perhaps you are jamming, scatting, rocking, rolling, jiving—creating your own music with others, or solo, on the fly or according to the charts.

Music almost always starts from inspiration, and your ultimate goal is to convey that feeling *through* you as the performer to your audience. And it's the same way for all performing artists, whether the message is to be communicated in music, dance, or words, whether you're a musician playing the music of any style or period; a conductor, dancer, actor, or speaker; a business leader, spiritual teacher or minister; or a poet, entertainer, politician, or even a gymnast. Most people who perform in front of the public do so in order to communicate a message *through* their bodies and/or their voices *so persuasively* that their message will inspire and empower their audience. Whenever we experience great performances by the most amazing performers, it is their message which touches us, not just the communicator to whom we express our gratitude and appreciation. It is the *message* that has the power—and as musicians and artists, we are the ones who are called upon to deliver this inspirational word or experience. However, I have personally observed that every time we get up onstage, we have the ability to deliver the entire message—or to filter, inhibit or perhaps altogether fail to do so.

We have many wonderful performers who can deliver messages of inspiration, excitement or beauty in a way that quite transcends their personalities. Have you ever watched Elvis Presley perform (or jazz pianist Oscar Petersen, opera singer Renee Fleming, the Turtle Island String Quartet, conductor Leonard Bernstein, singer/ conductor Bobby McFerrin or the Kronos Quartet)—or seen the now-famous YouTube clips of the Venezuela Youth Orchestra under their sensational young conductor Gustavo Dudamel? It's as though these great performers dissolve into the essence of the music they are making.

What do these super stars do that ordinary performers don't?

They perform with such energy and intensity you can actually see the muscles in their body—and they give themselves heart and soul to the music!

It goes without saying that these great performers have mastered *discipline*, *technique*, *intonation* (being in tune) and *musicianship*. Those are certainly skills that every aspiring musician will need to learn, practice and carefully master—but they are not what this book is about. You can do everything this book will show you and

4

it will be a total wash unless you bring integrity, sensitivity and scholarship to your performances.

In this book we explore the ways these great performers actually perform, watching their gestures and actions, then integrating what they do into a method of teaching, learning and expressing music so that it comes to life!

This book is about facilitating the magic—about channeling a thought, idea, experience or message through your art and yourself to the point where it transcends you. It's about reassessing how we communicate and perform, and even how we learn the techniques that we use in our performance. It will take us places we may never have dreamed of, and teach us skills we might not imagine would be helpful, let alone integral and indeed, essential to our artistic training. And at the same time it may carry us back to a natural innocence we once had and show us how to bring it into our adult world.

My own artistic and personal life has been permanently and positively changed by my recognition of the ways in which we use our bodies to communicate the life in music. I don't claim to be the first to discover this; I just claim to have been an honest observer.

Now let me talk to you on a more personal level—because these are matters which touch us all at the level of heart and soul. In my own journey, I've found that the great music moments happen when I am completely open about my feelings.

I want you to notice what happens when we are moved to tears by beauty or truth, when our breath is taken away, when we become speechless—when we reach the highest peaks of our experience or plunge most deeply into our soul, when we *feel* the most and show it, exposing our vulnerability to the fullest: we receive support rather than criticism, and love, not rejection.

The journey toward our innate and natural depth of feeling that I am proposing here isn't about overcoming anxiety this time. I showed you how to deal with those issues by means of the

Awareness, Commitment and Trust skills and exercises in *The Inner Game of Music*. In this book, the journey involves transforming our notions of what physical skills are central to preserving the spirit of an artistic message.

I can't simply wave a wand and mutter a magic formula over you; there aren't any shortcuts you can take to get where we're going; and you may, in fact, feel as though I'm leading you by a very roundabout path on occasion. But I intend to offer you a very convincing presentation of three key elements which greatly influence our ability to communicate and inspire those we perform for.

You cannot force your music to have that magical touch of inspiration; it doesn't work that way. But together we can create an environment that's inviting and musical. There are no guarantees, but the tools, techniques and pathways I present here, accompanied by patience, discipline and integrity, are liable to alter the way you perform and listen to others—permanently.

I'll give you a template to help you strengthen your inspiration and give new life to your performances.

From *The Inner Game of Music* via *The Mastery of Music* to *Bringing Music to Life*

I am a classically trained musician who has been playing the acoustic bass for more than forty years. I was Principal Bassist of the Cincinnati Symphony Orchestra for twenty-eight seasons, and my passion for music has also led me into writing books, teaching classes for musicians of all ages and genres, and performing and collaborating with artists in many, many different styles of music.

This is the third book in which I explore human elements outside the mainstream of classical music instruction.

My first book, with best-selling author Timothy Gallwey, applied Inner Game concentration techniques (which Tim first presented in *The Inner Game of Tennis*) to the making of music. *The Inner Game of Music* has sold over 250,000 copies worldwide, providing one of the primary means by which many musicians have overcome their mental obstacles to performance and learning. Like Tim's other *Inner Game* books, it explores the three master skills of Awareness, Commitment and Trust—and by disconnecting musicians from those doubts and fears which inhibit their performance, reconnects them to their music.

The Inner Game has not lost any of its power, luster or effectiveness. Human nature is ever-present, anxious to seize your attention and distract your performance—and we will always need the Inner Game skills to overcome these distractions.

After many years of practicing and teaching the Inner Game, though, I discovered that there were elements of excellence that were not included in my Inner Game work. This understanding led me to write *The Mastery of Music: Ten Pathways to True Artistry*. Here I explored the human spirit in such varied expressions as courage, confidence, passion, communication, joy, tolerance, creativity, humility and inspiration, drawing on more than 120 interviews with world-class musicians. I learned that it's not just what we play or how well we play the music, but more importantly, what special qualities we bring to our performance that give us our uniqueness.

The qualities named above that I explored in *The Mastery of Music* are central to the process by which each one of us develops our own unique voice.

In studying how great musical artists have mastered these human qualities I saw the great impact they can have on our own musicianship and life. Great artists constantly reinvent themselves and never stop growing, learning or reaching for excellence.

It was writing the final two chapters of *The Mastery of Music* on inspiration and creativity which led me into the terrain I am focusing on in this third book on the spirit and life in music—still on an endless journey born of my own curiosity toward the richest understanding of musical excellence and artistic fulfillment.

Comparing *The Inner Game* to *Bringing Music to Life*

In many ways, *Bringing Music to Life* is a lot like *The Inner Game of Music*. The Inner Game approach offers musicians a method for achieving optimum concentration and is primarily mental in its approach. It is based on three skills of concentration: Awareness, Commitment and Trust. *Bringing Music to Life* also presents a method, in this case, for communicating the sheer vitality, the *life* in music—but this time the techniques are applied to the body and soul of the performer. Both approaches can result in dramatically enhanced musical performances.

Bringing Music to Life also brings you three performance techniques, but these three have to do with body awareness rather than awareness of what the mind is up to. While *The Inner Game of Music* requires you to balance the three skills of Awareness, Commitment and Trust to achieve a state of relaxed concentration, *Bringing Music to Life* develops the three skills of Breath, Pulse and Movement, and integrates them in such a way as to bring *life* to music!

I wrote the Inner Game book after more than four years of research and testing Tim's principles with individuals and groups at a variety of levels and in a wide range of musical styles. I have likewise field-tested the principles of *Bringing Music to Life* with artists in diverse fields of popular and classical music, with young and mature musicians, in schools, music education and performance. And just as the Inner Game approach was based on and inspired by the methodology of Tim Gallwey's *Inner Game of Tennis*, the concepts developed in *Bringing Music to Life* have been largely based on and inspired by what I have seen of the method of renowned cellist, composer and educator, David Darling, of teaching free improvisation in his truly inspirational "Music for People" workshops.

Both books build on a cluster of natural principles which have been researched and codified so that they provide readers with a set of basic methods for approaching concentration and performance. Tim Gallwey's Inner Game has its roots in Eastern philosophy, and David Darling's Music for People is based on a return to the eager music making of childhood. His teaching method reflects accepted models of child pedagogy while it harkens back to indigenous folk cultures with their traditions of singing, dancing and drumming which have been with us as long as there have been human societies.

It all comes back to this: whether a piece of music has been composed or is being improvised in the moment, the composer or performer has felt the impulse to express something. The music may relate to a person, an occasion, some aspect of nature; it may tell a story, reflect a feeling such as love or beauty—or a passion for dance. Whatever this underlying thread of the work may be in any particular case, it is the performer's fortunate task to capture this inspiration, internalize it, and then pass it along through music, drama, dance or words. And we have the power to inhibit or refresh our understanding and internalization of this message as we receive it or as we transmit it back out into the world through our own bodies.

The Structure of This Book

I have written this book in three parts, each part containing three chapters. Part I presents the basic concept of the book: that when we integrate the three skills of Breath, Pulse and Movement, the body naturally becomes a vehicle for the inspiration which alone can bring our music to life. Part II presents these three techniques of Breath (Voice), Pulse (Rhythm) and Movement (Body) in detail, with exercises and anecdotes from great performers. And Part III explores the magic that emerges when a performance comes to life.

Part I: The Methodology

In Part I, the first chapter is called *Recapturing the Child* and is about returning to that youthful spirit for life and music. Chapter 2 is *A Recipe for Inspiration,* and reveals a physical "template" for the expressive performing artist. I will tell you about the great jazz bassist Rufus Reid and the impact one of his performances had on me; about a conference I attended where a group of fiddlers played classical and Irish folk fiddle; and about my own personal journey studying free improvisation with David Darling. Chapter 3, *Finding the Pathway,* chronicles the five years of developing a methodology for bringing music to life. As a work in progress never ends, it is a pathway that led to many exciting discoveries concerning refining and articulating the illusive elements that allow music to become alive.

Part II: The Three Techniques

Part II presents the three techniques of *Breath (Voice)* [chapter 4], *Pulse (Rhythm)* [chapter 5] and *Movement (Body)* [chapter 6]. I offer many activities that we can do at our own pace and in our own way to develop and integrate these three body-based skills. You will hear many experts from the world of voice, rhythm and movement share their insights to better understanding of how we can embrace their disciplines and incorporate them into our own performances. I hope you will be overwhelmingly convinced that these three skills are so essential to the essence of bringing music to life that you will continue to develop them in your own way.

Part III: Inspiration

Part III is directly devoted to our ultimate goal: the world of inspiration. In *The Complete Package* (chapter 7) we visit five incredible examples of music when it is alive in classical, rock and Latin music. We can see the ultimate template of Breath, Pulse and Movement in the bodies of Joshua Bell, the Kronos Quartet, Tito Puente, Leonard Bernstein and Gustavo Dudamel. The proof is in the product. It is obvious by observing, emulating and being inspired by these lively musicians.

Being in the Moment—It's You! (chapter 8) traces the inspiring stories of six of my colleagues who have found their own path to creating spontaneous moments that shimmer with musical life and spirit. Each of them has a unique voice and style, but they all strive for that improvisational moment where we find the magic in the music. Our final chapter, *Chasing the Rainbow* (chapter 9) explores the reasons artists dedicate their lives to pursuing the inspiration in music. What is the prize? Why do we do this? What are the feelings we are striving to have for ourselves and to share with others? And we learn that the joy is in the chase that inspires staying in the race and continuing to pursue the rainbow.

Although I recommend that you read this book from cover to cover, all three parts of this book stand alone and do not need to be read in sequence. If you are only interested in the techniques, then you can begin with Part II. If you like reading the books before going to the movies so you know the end result, then you can start with Part III! If you are a skeptic and need to be convinced of the premise and development of these concepts, then it will be important for you to begin with Part I! Otherwise, I believe there is a natural progression that flows from reading the book in sequence from Part I to the end.

Researching and Developing
Bringing Music to Life

First, let's talk about breath and voice. Breathing is a central discipline in yoga, meditation and tai chi, and each of these has added to my appreciation for breath as I learned a great deal about the voice from the celebrated author, composer and pianist W. A. Mathieu. I have also received brief but powerful individual coaching with voice teachers from both Eastern and Western styles of music, including Rhiannon, Silvia Nakkach, Lynn Miller, Kristin Korb and Douglas Webster.

I have learned about pulse and rhythm in depth while practicing and working with drummers and percussionists from a variety of world cultures, including Curt Moore, Kokomon Clottey and Masankho Kamsisi Banda, who was awarded the title of Unsung Hero of Compassion by the Dalai Lama—and have played jazz, improvisational, classical and world music with many Bay Area musicians.

And since so much of this book is about the body and movement, I have also taken introductory lessons in many types of movement discipline, from yoga and tai chi though jazz, hip-hop, *nia*, Eurythmics, Growth in Motion, energy work, Inter-Play, and even ballroom dancing. And for thirteen years, I have been developing movement sessions for musicians with Alan Scofield, the creative Bay Area dance teacher and choreographer from Young Imaginations.

In addition, I have done research and interviewed experts to supplement my own experiences. I attended David Darling's Music for People improvisation workshops for several years, applying his principles to different styles of music. His methods are described in the book from Music for People *Return to Child* by Jim Oshinsky. In 2005 I was able to conduct an experimental course called Inspiration in Music for all styles of music and musicians. The faculty included myself and my colleagues David Darling, the tai chi master Chungliang Al Huang, vocalist Rhiannon, famed educator Mary Knysh and choreographer Alan Scofield. This workshop helped me formulate the theoretical beginnings of this approach to performance.

Since then, I have been able to test the concepts in *Bringing Music to Life* through demonstrations at music conventions, college residencies and in short workshops, and to observe for myself just how it can best be passed on in the classroom, in the studio and onstage.

I am grateful to my private bass students and teaching colleagues at our annual Golden Gate Bass Camp for allowing us to integrate voice, rhythm and movement into the mainstream of the bass curriculum, working and playing jazz and classical music with over a hundred musicians of all ages. Indeed, the unique curriculum we developed at our Golden Gate Bass Camp from 2004–2008, while it was inspired by David Darling's free improvisation method, has proven successful when applied to many other styles of music and art.

For over five years, I have explored *Bringing Music to Life* concepts in some of the most established music education circles, working with new and veteran teachers at such institutions as VanderCook College in Chicago and developing an extensive, ongoing project in for various San Francisco Bay Area middle and high school music departments. And I have written a series of articles exploring my ongoing research for music journals and trade publications.

W. A. Mathieu wrote a special work called *Heart, Soul and Stomp*, integrating all the *Bringing Music to Life* concepts into a dramatic piece for strings. And my dear friend and colleague Don Campbell, author of *The Mozart Effect*, has been a consultant on this project since its inception and has offered many invaluable insights and resources.

Here's the Invitation

It doesn't matter why you are pursuing the arts, whether your reasons are personal, educational, spiritual or professional. At some deep and universal level, we all want to experience something extraordinary, beautiful, magical—something that inspires us and takes our breath away. What matters is that we realize we are indeed pursing the high joy that the arts can bring.

This isn't something we can force to happen—in fact, the harder we try, the less likely it is that the magic will appear. I am confident, though, that without opening up these three channels, we are liable to block, suffocate or inhibit our music from emerging with energy and freshness.

As we begin this journey of the observation and assimilation of Breath, Pulse and Movement into our performances, I believe you will also notice the contributing role these factors play in the great performances of Jimi Hendrix, Leonard Bernstein, Cab Calloway, Tina Turner or Yo-Yo Ma. Our image of these artists is one of movement and vital energy.

In the course of this book I will mention inspiration and spirit, time and again. After all, we are searching for inspiration, we all want to be thrilled, touched or moved in the core of our bodies and souls. Music has the undisputed power to heal, inspire, transform and transcend time and cultures, and indeed, in the final analysis, there may be no separation between the power that music has over our consciousness and our spiritual lives. The very nature of inspiration itself is something I look forward to exploring with you in the course of this book.

Be ready to let your hair down, feel your emotions—scat, move, groove, and jam. This is the approach that *Bringing Music to Life* proposes, and you can apply it to any style of music at any level of performance. It is the perfect way to capture the essence of the inspiration we receive from nature, from people, from life—and to share it with the world.

I can offer you hints and pathways. Ultimately, though, *you* will be the one who takes this journey and makes it your own.

Part I
The Methodology

Chapter 1
Recapturing the Child

I am mentally preparing myself for the five-year-old mind. I want to come down to their physical limitations, and up to their sense of wonder and awe.

—Shinichi Suzuki

Children make music for the sheer fun of it.

Children make music joyfully, instinctively, enthusiastically. They hum to themselves, they whistle, they skip and dance, drum their pencils on the table, and love to find out what sounds pots and pans make. Music comes naturally to them.

There comes a point, however, where music can become a task and even an obligation instead of a free expression of play, and that point may come when "music lessons" begin, or as "practice" becomes a looming necessity, like bad weather on the horizon. That's when the child's sense of music as play begins to shrink, when the enthusiasm begins to wane, and worries creep into the picture.

In my first book, *The Inner Game of Music*, I suggested some techniques that can help you sidestep the worries and play with the body's natural assurance. The more recent *The Mastery of Music* showed how different sides of human character from courage to passion can be expressed in music making.

Picasso once said, "All children are artists—the problem is how to remain artists once we grow up." In this third book, we will work together to recapture the child's enthusiasm for music, so that like a child, you can throw yourself body and soul into your music making, without worries, with character, and with a magical ingredient that I can't quite name but will call inspiration for now—with life, with spirit!

It was W. Timothy Gallwey, author of *The Inner Game of Tennis*, who provided the Inner Game structure which proved applicable to many other performance disciplines besides tennis, and which led to my writing *The Inner Game of Music*. I am grateful for the mentoring he gave me as I learned to apply his principles to music. In this book, I will pick up on the exploration of *inspiration* and *creativity* which I began in the final two chapters of *The Mastery of Music* and use exercises like those we explored in *The Inner Game of Music*. In this book we will rediscover the inspiration that childhood's innocence and joy bring to music making, then move forward into practice techniques and performance skills which can keep that inspiration alive—and this time, I am grateful to the great improvising cellist David Darling for his mentoring and philosophy.

David Darling, together with Music for People (the organization he co-founded), has developed a method of teaching "free improvisation" which has been a jumping-off point for my explorations of how our music making can really come to life— leading to this book, *Bringing Music to Life*. Like Tim Gallwey's Inner Game principles, David's principles of free improvisation are equally applicable not only to bringing all styles of music alive, but also to other performing arts such as dance and theater.

I began to study with David because I hoped to get a better understanding of the creative process—and thus figure out how to bring spontaneity not just to improvised music, but also to classical music. I have long felt that improvised music, folk music, jazz, rock, pop, and indeed almost any music that is learned and performed by ear has an energy and spirit not often found in those kinds of music we learn from reading sheet music.

At the very highest professional levels, yes, classical music, too, has that energy, that vitality—but for many of us, that sense of life gets lost somewhere along the way, worn down in part by the way we practice and in part by the seriousness of the music itself, of what we might call the "weight of the classics." And that's a great shame, because the great classics became classics because they were so full of life.

I'd very much like to turn that situation around, to make sure that when we're making music, we're always making music alive! And it seems to me that studying free improvisation is a simple, direct, and accessible way for us to enter a spontaneous, childlike musical world where that vital energy is naturally present—where for one thing, there are no "wrong notes"—so we can bring it into all of the music we make.

The Importance of Returning to Our Childhood State

Children love to play—and that goes for playing music as well as for playing other games.

As I have found in my teaching, young children naturally respond to song, dance and rhythms. And we love watching our children perform in youth ensembles or their school concerts. What I find especially enjoyable, though, is watching skilled youth ensembles playing with a sense of reckless abandon while still maintaining their technical proficiency.

It is possible to enjoy music making without the proficiency, to be sure, but it really adds to one's appreciation when it is present, and it often seems that when young musicians can't play very well they don't seem to be having much fun, either. I was reminded of this when I was in Nova Scotia and witnessed the youthful joy that exploded in the workshops David and I taught together on Inspiration in Music!

For me, returning to my own childhood was the critical first step in understanding how important it is for us all to recapture that childlike delight in making music. It was learning David's creative techniques for teaching free improvisation that made the difference for me. There are many paths and disciplines which can facilitate your own return to childhood, and most everyone can benefit from bringing their rediscovered, youthful enthusiasm into the adult world of artistic expression.

My Own Path Back

My own "return to childhood" caught me completely by surprise. I had no clue what was coming, and once it happened, I couldn't stop it. And that first experience remains a beacon for me, a reminder that the child I once was can revisit me at any time if I allow him to.

I was attending a week-long course in the Art of Improvisation led by David Darling in Fredonia, New York. I had chosen to attend this workshop because of my ongoing interest in the process of creativity, something which had fascinated me ever since I wrote the last two chapters of *The Mastery of Music*.

I had been attending weekly jam sessions as an amateur jazz player, playing numbers out of *The Real Book* with some highly skilled jazz colleagues, and it occurred to me that free improvisation—where there are no wrong notes and theory isn't so important—might teach me a great deal more about the creative process itself.

Free improvisation offered me a more friendly environment for self-expression than jamming over complex jazz harmonies to tunes I didn't know very well. But that wasn't all. Darling's method of teaching improvisation not only showed me how to "return to my own child" and experience once again the childlike delight that had drawn me into music in the first place—it also helped me make his principles and practices my own so that I could explore and develop their use with other styles of music.

Returning to My Childhood at Music for People

It was the summer of 2004. I was attending David Darling's Art of Improvisation course in Fredonia, New York. I was in a room with more than eighty musicians of all ages, all walks of life, and all levels of musical training, from complete beginners to symphony professionals—myself included!

Now, how in the world could all these people possibly make music together? The magic of my experience at this workshop was that they not only did it, they did it more often, with more vitality, sheer electricity and inspiration than I was used to when playing with highly trained professional musicians. To be honest, I expect that perhaps twenty percent of the times I play with my professional peers and colleagues, whether from the jazz, classical, folk or chamber music traditions, we'll experience one of those moments in music when everything comes together. And yet here I was with a quite varied bunch of amateur improvisers, and that kind of special excitement was at work about eighty percent of the time! Something was drastically different here—but it was no accident!

Here's how it worked.

One of David's keys to improvisation had me spending a whole lot of time *away* from my bass, getting back into the swing of some things I used to do as a kid. Act, he says, like the child you once were. And I did. I sang, danced around, banged on anything and everything that could make a sound! And I must tell you, I loved acting absolutely crazy (like a kid!) with my voice, hands and bass—then screaming at the top of my lungs. I saw David wear many faces as he was working with us—but the one face I never saw was that of the pompous virtuoso-master teacher. Pomposity just isn't in his playbook.

David's coaching style involves simple imitation. First he sings it, shouts it, plays it, demonstrates it, and then we follow. It is so easy to do. And it really is designed to evoke some amazing and amazed group responses—laughter, love, some pretty high-level exaltation, even some freaking out.

Darling's Mantras

David has what he calls Mantras. He shouts out "Mantra 1" or "Mantra 2" and that's the signal for us all to respond.

Mantra 1 is where everyone has to laugh at themselves, or at least smile. It may sound like nothing special, but believe me, this can be *huge*. We cannot and must not take ourselves seriously when we do something stupid or funny. Adults get upset, embarrassed and perhaps angry on these occasions—and how can you make music when you're feeling like that? Kids laugh at themselves all the time. When kids stumble or fall down, they don't get mad, they get up and keep on going.

Laughter is a wonderful medicine for the spirit—and for your health too! So that's Mantra 1: laugh at yourself, don't get mad, laugh!

David's Mantra 2 is *Oooohh!* Imagine holding a baby bird in your hands, a bird so small that your hands are folded right over it— and when you open your hands to take a look at the bird, it chirps… That's *Oooohh!* Mantra 2 represents sheer energy, an expression of the awe and amazement we feel when something totally incredible takes place. It is the miracle of life. And that kind of breathtaking is the essence of an awe that we can pass along to our audience when we experience it. If you really understand it right, Mantra 2 really cuts to the core of "returning to the child"—every thing, every moment, every note, every sound is a gift.

It is amazing. It is special. Life is special.

When David says: "Mantra 1," we all make the appropriate response as a group: we laugh! And it's a really wonderful infectious feeling. And Mantra 2 reminds us to appreciate being and playing together, and creating sounds that can make music alive.

Freaking Out

One of the highlights of David's course was learning how to *freak out!*—how to act like a complete child, but with your instrument or voice! Plain old going crazy was another way he would lead us back into total immersion in the music. Think of a rock star or two. Those folks do this all the time! A football player celebrating a touchdown, an athlete who has just broken the ribbon! They freak out! We need to do this ourselves. It's part of the script for the human body—that sense of abandonment, of release!

It was the most amazing thing to me, when something would start building a musical phrase and we could all let it really go wild. It's really shameful, in my opinion, that the mind holds so much energy in check because of our sense of tradition or reputation, or because we're so keen to "be in control"—when instead, we could just let it *hang out*.

Egoless Participation

When David set the ground rules for the week, he included egoless participation and talked about *listening*—in fact, he told us that this was the master skill we would study the most. It's not what we play that counts in music, it's the music we're making together. And I learned that one of the keys to improvisation is not what or when to play, but when *not* to play. And we learn this by listening.

More of Darling's improvisation techniques can be found in *Return to Child* by James Oshinsky, the Music for People manual for improvising music (available at www.musicforpeople.org).

My Own Return

My breakthrough return to childlike enthusiasm and delight took place during an improvisation exercise. In that particular session I felt a very emotional reconnection to my bass while surrounded by many supportive and loving colleagues.

We were improvising in a circle, and each of us in turn was asked to play a solo and end on a sustained note—and this would be the cue for the next person to solo and for the previous one to provide the background for it. So the solo moves around the circle, and the background builds as each person in turn plays. I was near the end of the circle, so when it was my turn to solo there was already a richly textured and sustained chord in the air to serve as the backdrop for my improvisation. It got closer and closer to my turn to solo and my emotions were beginning to overwhelm me—I just had no sound prepared. I felt almost paralyzed.

Interestingly and perhaps not coincidentally, the person soloing immediately before me was the dancer Barbara Feldman-Stein. She was moving around in the center of the circle. It was really beautiful, and I didn't want to play while she was dancing to the soothing sounds of the group. Barbara seemed to be dancing around the circle with her hands a few feet above the floor, as if there was an invisible rail she was resting them on. I wanted to join her, but I didn't know how.

I moved my bass to the center of the room, putting it on its side and sat there next to it on the floor. This allowed me to pluck the strings below the bridge or tap percussive sounds on the side and back of the bass. Quite soon, Barbara joined me in tapping the bass. It felt as though my bass was the focus for this beautiful attention, and I half expected everyone else might join Barbara and myself in the circle with their hands playing percussion sounds on my bass—and all of a sudden I noticed I was there by myself. Even Barbara had somehow disappeared.

While this was going on, there was a beautiful kaleidoscope of sounds in the air—each person there was playing a sustained note, and together they were producing a beautiful harmony, with some added color from the percussion instruments. And under it all was the rich drone of a didgeridoo. The whole texture felt soothing, even loving—and all of a sudden I felt as if the loving was being directed toward me, and wondered whether this was like the rhythm of life that a child hears in the womb.

I didn't really know what to do at this point. I felt unprepared to receive so much attention when I wasn't even really playing my bass. My breathing became very light, and I found myself silently gasping for air as my eyes filled with tears.

I hadn't played any notes to speak of—but my bass and I received a lot of loving attention and musical energy. This rather silent bass solo—just being present in the center of the circle—was the gift of the musical community that surrounded me.

I really didn't understand the emotion that welled up in me. I didn't realize at first that I had experienced a return to childhood in my own way—and that my return *of course* included this loving connection with my bass and music. It had been a long time since I had felt this way—I had forgotten how much I loved music, my bass and my musical voice.

I found myself embracing the bass as if I had neglected her. So many years had passed since I had felt this love for music, this freedom to express myself with my bass, this love from friends and colleagues. But now I had come back. Through that passage of love and emotion I had returned to the childlike passion I had for music when I first started to play the bass. I was home again.

I didn't know it at the time, but I realize in retrospect the whole process really was a celebration, even though it was also an exhausting, emotional, and somewhat embarrassing experience for me. It was only later, when I heard my friends in the circle expressing their gratitude for what had happened to me that I fully realized it was *okay* to be so vulnerable.

And that's all part of what David meant by that phrase of "egoless participation." I can see that now. It is okay, it is more than okay, it is a very positive thing to allow your emotions to come through—even if you're used to holding them back, to keeping them in check, and you feel embarrassed and vulnerable.

The Importance of Allowing Emotions

There have been many times since that day when I have felt overcome by emotion while making music—and each time, I come back to that experience in the circle with my bass. I learned then that as artists, we must be prepared to show our emotions, all our emotions, to set them free. If we hold them back like "mature" adults, we are filtering our inspiration. We may think we are acting cool and professional—but our audience doesn't want a filtered experience, people don't want the feeling in the music they hear to be censored! If we hold ourselves back, we are shortchanging our public.

This issue would crop up again many more times over the five years it took me to develop the principles and exercises in *Bringing Music to Life*. High School students in particular *really* don't want to act like kids; they want to be *cool*. Adults want to be admired and envied for their accomplishments and what they do, but young kids don't care. They express themselves exactly the way they feel. They go crazy with excitement. They cry with abandon. And we love them for it.

If we stop feeling embarrassed about showing our emotions, we can get excited as we make music, we can weep, we can become transparent, playful—and amazed at the beauty of the sounds we make. *Oooohh!* It will be another one of David's Mantra 2 moments!

Each of us has to find our own way to return to the child—to return to our own child—and embracing this return is a *necessary part of our artistry*. Whether it's a tender emotional return or a sudden unleashing of spontaneous silliness, we each need to find our way back and stay connected with the inspiration that brings such youthful life to our music.

In that process, David's two mantras—laughing at ourselves, and feeling the *Oooohh!* of wonder—can be our daily companions.

From Child to Adult

As children grow older, their parents and teachers become more serious about them *making progress*—which often results in the children having less fun. Grades, competitions and performances become the focus. The children must learn to read music. They must *specialize*! And the cycle continues as they get older. As fast as they acquire advanced skills their parents and teachers acquire advanced expectations.

Young musicians may experience the pressures of auditions or competitions on an amateur or professional level. Suppose they are successful in keeping music as a part of their lives—do they still maintain their youthful joy of learning and playing for the sheer pleasure of musical experience? As our youth dissolves into adulthood, it is only too possible to forget what brought us to our art in the first place. Our joy and play can become distant memories. If we can take the time to go back, if we can use our memories as a time machine, we can bring that joy forward into our adult world and play with the same energy and vitality that we had when we started.

You may remember the day when you transitioned from playing by ear, the "aural tradition" of the Suzuki approach, to the "printed tradition" and began to focus your efforts on the accurate re-creation of the notes and symbols on a page. One of my mentors as I explore the magical elements of music is William Allaudin Mathieu, the great composer and pianist, and author of the famous *Listening Book*. Allaudin has helped me understand the difference between two styles of music by labeling them *hot* and *cool*.

He told me:

> The way I see it, music is either *hot* or *cool*—by which I mean it either comes directly from inside of us without benefit of notation (like jazz and other improvised music) or it originates externally—from a composer like Beethoven, for instance—and we internalize it by means of reading notation. The direct process from inside out I call *hot*. The music comes straight out of our own juices. The intervention of notation *cools* the process, while providing us with an opportunity for deep intellectual play—as, for

instance, in the case of Bach. I love both ways of music making, each has its own glory. And I have spent a lifetime looking for recipes for compromise and accommodation between them.

The question in terms of classically trained musicians then becomes: How can we introduce musicians to both aspects of music at once so they can meet the demands of direct emotional connection in the moment while also reading difficult ensemble music off the page?

My experience watching master teachers of improvisation has helped me identify those missing musical elements which the printed page so easily obscures. They are the same musical elements that help us overcome external pressures and the social demands placed on maturing and competing professional musicians. I have studied improvisation and also observed performing musicians of all levels and styles from classical to folk, and it is not difficult to notice that the most spirited music making is free of all these adult impositions.

Child on the Inside, Adult Outside

You have probably noticed the same kind of joyous music making yourself. Have you ever watched the Turtle Island String Quartet, the Kronos String Quartet, Hector Lavoe, Yo-Yo Ma and the Silk Road musicians, the Philadelphia Orchestra, or seen Leonard Bernstein conducting? Take a moment to visit YouTube to experience Gustavo Dudamel conducting the Venezuelan Youth Orchestra in Bernstein's *Mambo* from West Side Story (http://www.youtube.com/watch?v=6yjcfnkubjq. If the link is dead, search YouTube for Venezuelan Youth Orchestra Mambo). Have you ever seen violinist Joshua Bell, or the New Orleans trumpet great Louis Armstrong, or jazz pianist Oscar Petersen?

What excites me about all these performers is that even if you couldn't hear the glorious sounds they are making, they all look remarkably similar! You can *see* that they are all pouring heart and soul *through* their bodies *into* the music.

And this is the key!

When you can *see* all three elements—Breath, Pulse and Movement—you *feel spirit.*

The look they all share is one of youthful maturity. They are childlike adults! They are totally absorbed in the moment and the experience they are having, they are alive and full of energy.

It is the adult's true dream to be able to feel, act and play like a child—while at the same time using our experience, intellect and advanced physical skills. That way we can be children on the inside and present ourselves as adults on the outside.

This is the look of mastery. This is the look of a Picasso, of an Einstein.

Maintaining the Youthful Approach

And the secret to maintaining this youthful approach?

It all begins with the body.

I have found there are many ways in which we limit, block or interfere with our inspiration. *Allowing ourselves to be one hundred percent available to our inspiration involves learning where in our bodies we block it, and how to allow the message to flow through us.* And that means we must look to the body itself to find ways to remove those blocks. That's where this book can help. That's where Breath, Pulse and Movement enter the picture.

It's up to *you!* The music has to come *into* your body, heart, soul and mind, and flow back out *through* you. You are alive and unique. You will give the music your own feeling, spirit, accent, flavor, pulse, sound and groove. But first you must take care not to obstruct your inspiration.

A Natural Exploration

I must warn you from the beginning: the journey we will be taking is not a direct upward path for any performing artist—there will be highs and lows, setbacks and also moments of true wonder. There is a natural progression that will unfold here, and patience will play its role. While there is no doubt that gifted young artists can sometimes achieve stardom, our pathway to the promised lands of artistry will be the richer for a mature understanding that springs from our personal growth and discipline.

When I was in high school, I remember Walter DeCloux, our conductor, telling the members of the all-state orchestra that music was *"a beautiful painting on a background of silence."*

That striking phrase has stuck with me throughout my musical career, and now it reminds me how important it is to master *The Inner Game of Music,* so that by knowing and using the principles of concentration you can manage the inner chatter and steer clear of mental distractions. We cannot afford to be paralyzed by doubts and fears, by confusion and lack of discipline, when we are pouring heart and soul into our music.

And we also know that every day presents new challenges to our mental skills. Lao Tsu, the sixth century BCE Chinese poet who is credited as the father of that great little book, the *Tao Te Ching,* wrote:

Empty yourself of everything. Let the mind become still. The ten thousand things rise and fall while the Self watches their return. They grow and flourish and then return to the source. Returning to the source is stillness: this is the way of nature.

It seems the first step to learning anything is letting go of what you already know so that you can absorb something new as fully as possible. It is very important, I believe, for us to retrace our youthful experiences with music so we can figure out what worked and where things went astray.

When a performer brings emotional baggage of any kind—doubt, judgment, hesitation, ego, expectation, self image—onto the stage, it will be as though the music has been filtered though it. It is no longer coming from silence.

And the beauty of youth is that at first, there is none of this history, none of this baggage to get in the way… There is no judgment; just innocence and enthusiasm, nothing but total being and presence.

Miles Davis said: *Don't play what's there, play what's not there.*

First Love

First love is a timeless experience, and first love in music often comes at a point where you've achieved a level of proficiency that allows you some freedom to express yourself. But you do not have to have all the technical virtuosity in the world to experience the grace and beauty of music. I have seen and participated many times under David Darling's direction in his Music for People sessions, watching a trained professional symphonic cellist improvise with an untrained eleven-year-old percussionist, an amateur singer, and someone sitting at the piano who has never had a formal lesson. And let me assure you: magic can happen when these diverse groups of artists let themselves be inspired as they play together.

It is the individuals' participation which gives this kind of group experience the possibility of greatness. Allowing space for the silence between the notes is also important. And there are elements of form, structure, communication, emotion and respect for others which can help build this delicate yet passionate state of excitement in any performance.

I have watched the magic happen time and again, and I have noticed that there's a physical template for the kind of awareness that facilitates this kind of magic in our performances. It's a template consisting of three techniques which we'll explore in the next chapter.

In *Bringing Music to Life* we are mastering three new principles which lead directly to inspiration. And wherever we are in our artistic journey, we need to approach these powerful techniques with one-hundred percent of our energy and with childlike abandon.

Whether I'm at a pop concert, watching the Cirque du Soleil, or even at a sporting event, I've noticed that a performance that shows less than a one-hundred percent effort is greeted with boos and disdain—even in the world's great opera houses, even when the performers are all dressed up in black tie and tails.

Just assembling a lot of technically proficient musicians who want to try hard onstage doesn't ensure anything. But I've noticed that when I see a one-hundred percent effort accompanied by a rich balance of Breath, Pulse and Movement—the three principles of *Bringing Music to Life*—that's when the spontaneous youthful spirit of the music has the best chance to emerge.

Music has a life of its own.

You can prepare for it, you can know your instrument and know your notes—but the magic in music cannot be scripted, it cannot be dictated, you cannot force it. It has its own life, and its own way of making itself heard. The best way we can prepare to make magical music is to have all our physical and mental channels open and available. And the way to do that is to open up the three aspects of our being which form the core of this book: Breath, Pulse and Movement.

That's when inspiration takes over, when the pure, youthful virtuoso emerges and truly brings our music to life!

Chapter 2
A Recipe for Inspiration

Jay Greenberg may well be the new Mozart.

Jay was twelve years old when I saw him on a recent CBS *Sixty Minutes* program. He's already written five full-length symphonies, and he's studying music with some of the very best at New York's renowned The Juilliard School. Some highly respected classical musicians say he is the greatest composing talent to come along in 200 years: "We are talking about a prodigy of the level of the greatest in history," says composer Sam Zyman. "I am talking about the likes of Mozart, and Mendelssohn, and Saint-Saens."

And Jay Greenberg? What does he have to say for himself?

Greenberg says music just fills his head, and to get it out, he has to write it down. Like Mozart, he says he hears his music all at once, and when he takes the time to write it down, it comes through without revisions, it's already complete. One piece called "The Storm" he wrote in just a few hours. That's impressive in itself. But it is when Jay was asked *how* he hears his music, that I really found his answer was truly profound. Jay explained that he likes to be walking!

That's right. When he hears the music, he engages his *body*, he conducts the music he is hearing, and he sings along as he is conducting it! He's walking, singing and playing (conducting) it simultaneously! Hang on to that thought—because this is the state of being in which Jay receives his most creative inspiration—like Mozart before him. In the now-celebrated letter in which Mozart describes his preferred ways of composing, he, too, says that taking a walk can help.

There's a temptation to put Mozart up on a pedestal, and Jay too, perhaps, but I'd like to avoid that and to focus instead on what these brilliant composers can teach us about what comes naturally to them—making music.

Have you even been stuck at your desk with a tricky math problem or some other challenge, and felt like getting up and walking around a bit? As you pace up and down, or go for a stroll round the block, there's a rhythm you fall into, you "hit your stride." And have you noticed that when you do this, sometimes—*boom*—the answer comes to you, the solution just pops into your head?

Body and mind are not two separate entities, and I suggest to you that *we will find a far more powerful connection to the magic in music when we integrate the rhythms of our breath, pulse and bodily movements into our practice and performance.*

Inspiration and Creative Expression Go through the Body

In my last book, *The Mastery of Music*, I interviewed composer Terry Riley, one of the founding fathers of New Age music. Riley suggested that the source of all musical inspiration is a universal spirit or consciousness that we all can tap into. Riley believes there's a field of consciousness that somehow connects the whole universe, including ourselves, in one seamless web. We can find variations on the same idea in the writings of many religions and creative people, and whether or not you take it literally, we can agree to call the place where ideas arise in awareness within us our own consciousness, awareness or intuition. It's the wellspring, the source of inspiration.

Now it seems to me that a creative genius like Mozart has an exceptionally finely tuned antenna for this kind of thing. He can pick up signals from the "consciousness" station much better than most of us—but we can tune into that station, too.

Is inspiration available to everyone, and do we simply differ in our individual ability to receive it? Can we improve our capacity to hear and respond to the same inspiration source that Mozart tuned into?

I believe that creativity is a byproduct of inspiration: first we need to channel an insight, an idea, or a sound, and then we need to convert that impulse into action. I find it fascinating to explore what we can do to make ourselves capable of hearing musical inspiration, and am convinced we can find many ways to convert that inspiration into a creative product through teaching, imaginative playing or improvising. For me, that's the order we need to work in. First capture the inspiration, then turn it into the making of music!

And what I've learned about inspiration and creativity in music appears to have equal application to all the fine arts: dance, theater, literature and even the visual arts, painting and sculpture. I have noticed that the integration of different mind-body activities (singing and dancing, acting and dancing, acting and singing, drawing and playing an instrument and so on) seem to help enormously both with receiving inspiration and in translating that inspiration into highly creative artistic expressions of many kinds.

Breathing Inspiration

Inspiration: did you know that the word quite literally means "breathing in"? Breathing in is inspiration, breathing out is expiration, and the hopes that sustain you while you're alive and breathing are your aspirations—if you're breathing along with someone as you plot some nefarious deed together, you're conspiring, and what you're up to is a conspiracy—and the basic idea behind the word in each of these cases is breath, which in Latin is *spiritus*, spirit.

So inspiration is a *spirited* state to be in, and its essence is breathing.

It all begins with the breath and silence.

I was reminded of this basic truth most recently when I attended one of David Darling's improvisation workshops. David taught us a preparation exercise that he insisted we practice before we began any improvisation. We took a deep breath, raised our hands above our heads as we inhaled, then let our hands slowly fall to our instruments as we exhaled. After a brief period of silence, and as inspiration came to us, we began to play.

This turned out to be one of the most important things I learned about the creative process. The silence inspired my fingers to move without my thinking about it and commanding them. I wasn't deciding, I was following my inspiration.

What I was learning, I later realized, was to enjoy the space and silence before I played—and even during my playing. I was learning to wait for the moment when my fingers would move by themselves. I'll have to admit that patience has never been my virtue—but here it was, quickly becoming my friend.

I'll let David tell you about this state of patient, alert silence in his own words, drawn from an interview with Jim Oshinsky in the Music for People book, *Return to Child*. He describes it as "sitting quietly, paying attention to what sounds come from the exhale when you pay attention to your breath...."

That exhale is our magic, that's the connection to the Infinite. The form comes out of actually sitting quietly, doing nothing, having no purpose and then taking a breath. In our connection to the universe, you let the sounds come out and then listen deeply to how it feels to you. And when one is able to receive this process in such a way that one is not negative, but one is just listening, that listening experience will change one's life.

Little did I know at the time that this experience was guiding me in my pursuit of the source of the *spirit* in music. By patient attention in this silence we can pick up on unconscious hints and possibilities which reveal their magic in the most beautiful and creative ways— through improvisation, in our music making and in our lives.

Your Body is the Vessel for Your Creativity

Your body is not only a responsive "receiver" for the spirit of music; it also processes and transforms it through some form of expression into what we call Art with a big "A"—music, dance, and so on. Chungliang Al Huang, the world famous tai chi master who is also a poet, educator, dancer and expert calligrapher, told me at our 2004 Inspiration in Music Workshop in Oakland California:

Reach up to the sky. As you reach up, remember to allow the energy to come down into you and bring you inspiration. If you reach for it and are open to it, it will come to you. The opposite way is to bring energy up from the earth, a grounding energy, and then all around you there's the middle, the human energy. Gather all of these energies into yourself, and you will never burn out.

Chungliang explained to me that in the Chinese way of viewing the world, there is fire energy, water energy (which is cleansing), and tree energy which reaches into the earth… and he taught me

41

to *release what you have, and make room for more.* Each form of energy comes from a different source: fire, earth, water, metal, and wood (the five Chinese elements), and each energy has a different sound, a different sensibility to contribute to your music.

Fire can represent youthful passion and energy. Water energy flows like a river, responding to different circumstances, fluidly adapting in speed and intensity—this flexibility can express itself in pulse or tempo. In the air we can hear birds singing and learn something of melody and harmony. The earth is our nurturing foundation, the grand structure that brings its vibration into our bodies and spreads it through our limbs—it must enter your body and fill you—and then be released.

"The wind of God is always there," Chungliang tells me, "you must learn to put out your sail and catch that wind; it will be of no use to you unless you are open to that which is greater than you."

And this, I believe, is where each one of us can be our own worst enemy. We don't always know how to allow the inspiration in, so we create blocks in our bodies that make it difficult for us to let go of our existing artistic ideas and see what else the silence may bring.

Multi-skill Integration

In the fall of 2004 I was invited to present a series of lectures at the Nova Scotia Music Educators Conference in Canada. Part of the conference featured a local showcase marathon concert with an array of public school ensembles: bands, orchestras, choruses, jazz groups, chamber groups, flute choirs, drum and fife corps—and step dancers! Celtic music is a huge presence in Nova Scotia, where Irish music is right up there with jazz combos in the schools, and there's a fiddle in most everyone's Cape Breton-Victoria house. The students in the bands and string ensembles were mostly trained in reading music while carefully following their fine conductors. The choirs sang pretty well, but seemed to get more animated when their bodies "joined in" with some simple hand gestures or footsteps. Their music making was good—but it wasn't "off the charts."

Then I saw something I will remember forever. I saw four young middle-school girls doing Irish step dancing.

Step dancing is the forerunner of today's Irish dancing, and it dates back to the dance masters of 1750. These dance teachers typically traveled a circuit within a single county, teaching their repertoire of dance steps and participating in competition with other dance masters.

These four girls not only danced, they sang while they danced—and two of them played the flute and fiddle, too! It struck me that here again, we have dance, playing and singing, all happening at the same time—and when *all these activities happen at once*, creative inspiration goes through the roof!

And the excitement was palpable, even when they weren't singing and playing. You could see the joy in their faces as they walked on- and offstage, there was a swagger to their walk—they lit up the room, and they made my day, my month and my year!

Three-skill Integration in the Creative Process

After I'd spent several years exploring music that includes the integration of Breath, Pulse and Movement I attended an outstanding concert which validated my sense of how important these factors really are.

It was 2005, and I was at the International Society of Bassists convention in Kalamazoo, Michigan. My colleague, the great jazz bassist, composer and educator Rufus Reid, presented a new work for nine musicians called *Linear Surroundings*. It included a vocalist who didn't sing words but vocalized as though her voice was another thread in a tapestry of instruments.

The music was a good crossover blend between classical, folk, jazz and world musics. There were no program notes, just movement titles like *Shadow Chasing, Moods, The Peaceful Flame* and *Collage*. The overall stylistic influence was a fusion of classical and jazz—the kind that's composed and notated, but with touches of improvisation. The musical spirit was quite compelling, and the musicians really reached their audience. I'd say this music was *deep*! The piece was brilliant!

The whole concert was packed, so I looked for a spot for myself and wound up standing at ground level between two large risers and listening from there. It was in that strange corner of the musical universe that I had my epiphany about the integration of body with spirit in music. My somewhat unusual point of view, standing there between the bleachers, allowed me to watch and listen to this music in a new way, and I found myself appreciating why some performers were more effective in their music making than others.

Some of these players had more jazz or classical training than others. I noticed that some of the more experienced jazz musicians appeared to be more "into their bodies" while others seemed stiff—and I got the clear impression that the fluid players were playing from their bodies and the stiff ones from the intellect. And here's the thing: the ones who were clearly comfortable grooving to the rhythm, whose bodies were full of subtle movements as though they might break into dance at any moment, had by far the greatest musical impact. The singer's body was alive with music as she vocalized, and seeing her next to a clarinet player, it was clear that the clarinetist, too, was singing with both instrument and body language—and if he hadn't had his mouthpiece in his mouth, he too might have well been singing.

And then there was the classically trained instrumentalist who was just sitting there, reading her part, playing the notes right, but... just not really into it, and her tone was dull and uninspiring, too.

Bottom line: I saw there was a direct link between those musicians whose whole being, both soul and body, moved with the flow of the rhythm, and the audience they were playing for. And those musicians whose bodies were not in touch with the rhythm of the music weren't touching their audience, either.

Once I noticed this powerful relationship between an audience and those performers who integrate their body (Breath, Pulse and Movement) into their music making, I began to look for it everywhere. I watched jazz, chamber music, orchestral, choral and band concerts at all levels of music making and all ages. And I found the same relationship of body involvement and power of music.

Other cultures know all about this! Members of the world's indigenous cultures don't learn songs on paper. Emotion, movement, comes from both mind and body. They sing, dance and play flutes and drums in tribal rituals and everything—storytelling, music, religion, family, culture—it is all one.

My five-year-old grandson spent much time with his nanny-grandmother, a former ballet star who still teaches dance. She plays my grandson CDs of musicals and dances for him every day. When he is in a restaurant and hears music, he stands right up and starts dancing and babbling away. He jams on an electronic keyboard to a computerized rhythm section and dances and sings while he plays the keys. This is just one happy baby at play. And apart from the fact that his bassist grandfather thinks he's great, there's nothing special about it—he's just a kid having fun.

And that's how it is, that's how music, and inspiration, and voice, and instruments, or even our pots and pans and pencils or tapping feet just naturally work together! It all comes through the body. When the body flows, the energy flows, and when the body is interrupted, the energy is interrupted.

Great performances in sports, dance and music require a rare level of intensity. I propose that this is *invariably* linked with total body involvement that has some sort of fluid, rhythmic singing quality. I invite you to see whether in your own experiences—whether in making music, seeing it performed, or in your most musical memories—this close connection with voice and body is there or not.

Eastern Disciplines that Integrate Mind, Body and Spirit

Darling has collaborated with tai chi master Chungliang Al Huang at the Esalen Institute for more than twenty-five years. In musical terms, after watching Chungliang, I have come to think of tai chi as a sort of continuous flow of unheard music from its source of inspiration somewhere out there in the cosmos, through the body, and back out to the cosmos again. That may sound very California, but in tai chi, Chinese, and Eastern terms in general, it makes a lot of sense.

You can recognize the influence of Chungliang's tai chi philosophy in Darling's style of communicating the spirit of music and life. And I have had the pleasure of watching Darling closely, many times, and his musical expression passes through his body in just the way I'm describing it.

If the Body is Stiff and Unyielding, It Cannot Express Life

Lao Tsu was one of China's great philosophers, and he said something that I find to be very profound indeed:

> Humans are born gentle and weak, but they're hard and stiff when they're dead; young plants are tender and full of sap, but in the end they are withered and dry—here's the difference: whatever is stiff and unbending is death's disciple, and by the same token, whatever is gentle and yielding is a disciple of life.

This philosophical poem from two thousand five hundred years ago and six thousand miles away may seem quite distant from modern-day thinking—but here it is, confirming exactly what I'd been noticing myself in terms of music making! If the body is stiff and unyielding, it cannot express life.

Chungliang Al sometimes talks about the ideogram of the emperor in Chinese calligraphy, which consists of three horizontal lines representing the heavens, the human realm and the earth, with a vertical line bringing them all together. "If you can connect these three realms," he told me, "you are a ruler of the essence of life." But how do you get to hold the sky energy, the energy of heaven?

> Open yourself, watch it come in and fill this life as spirit, as breath. And then it comes out through your body. We keep filling up with it and emptying it out into the world as love and sound and life. It is like food for our soul, spirit and body. We are free to receive this inspiration and transform it into music, art, movement and life.

It is breath (which the Chinese think of as of chi energy) and voice that connect the human spirit with any external instrument. Your voice—and this part is important—*whether it sings silently or aloud*, participates and joins the musical product. If voice and breath are blocked or silent, then the chi/spirit cannot move through your body into your musical instrument.

Darling leads exercises that connect the voice with the body in simple re-circulating movements derived from tai chi. When he makes the sound of a simple pizzicato note, he imagines it as part of the flow of a giant circle of energy and motion: it comes from sky or earth, it enters and leaves his body (and cello), and travels back out across the earth and up into the sky. It breathes with chi, with life energy.

Go out there under the wide sky, breathe and embrace all these elements, taking their spirit into your entire body. The body is the center, the heart of all this vital energy and knowledge. When the body is free and unblocked, the spirit will express itself in many ways: through dance, voice, fingers, instruments and even silence.

There are no limits to our inspiration apart from the limits of our imagination.

Vocalist Rhiannon Gets Inspiration through Her Body

Rhiannon is a musical sensation, known worldwide for her gift of singing, who has taught and performed with Bobby McFerrin in the Voicestra, his unique twelve-piece improvisational vocal orchestra. Watching Rhiannon at our 2005 Inspiration in Music Workshops, I marveled at how she could build musical layers into a complex tapestry of spontaneous grooves and appreciated how she arrived at each individual melody. Having spent time with Chungliang, I quickly noted that her body acts like a giant antenna tuned into earth and sky. The musical groove seems to travel through her body, finding its form and shape as it prepares to leave her body.

The singers or instrumentalists that stand in a large circle around her are divided into four or five groups. Rhiannon starts with a simple groove pattern, perhaps using just a few pitches. Rather than snapping her fingers in time or counting off out loud, she shows the tempo with her body. Then she begins to articulate a few more intricate patterns that might work with this groove, but others do not pick up on these more detailed patterns *until* she signals that she has figured it out. She says things like: "I'm working on it. Not yet." She tries out different sounds and rhythms, her hips swaying, her legs trembling. Then she says: "It's almost there" and continues to sway her hips.

Next, her shoulders and head engage in the groove as she feels it, and finally she sings it, repeating it several times until it is clear she has arrived at her final pattern. Then she repeats the process with the next group, feeling out another layer of the music and continuing around the circle. And you have the sense that the music comes into her from the earth and sky, rising through her feet, legs, hips, torso and shoulders, only to emerge through her voice when it is fully formed...

We are witnessing Chungliang's circle of chi once again.

Integrating the Pulse, Body and Voice through Drumming

The music educator, multi-instrumentalist, and vocalist Mary Knysh led sessions on creative music making and integrating vocal syllables with body/hand movements at my 2005 Inspiration in Music course. It didn't matter whether people were using sticks, boomwhackers, voice, body percussion or instruments—Mary made the external instruments disappear as she connected us to our inner music in a non-thinking state.

She showed us African drum language translated into pitched vocal and body percussion, *Goon Doon* (thighs), *Go Do* (stomach) and *Pah Tah* (clap), and then the Indonesian sounds of *Ta ki ta*, which are combined with steps, claps and the voice. If we listen and dance to the movements and rhythms of various cultures we see how each culture in turn integrates voice, body, rhythm and spirit into one sound. *Sing-dance-play* is all one fluid thing in these cultures—I wish we had a word for it. I wonder why our Western culture, with its reliance on mind and its neglect of body and voice, has cut us off so severely from our natural ability to make magical, full-bodied music.

Don't get me wrong—I know that the Kodaly, Orff, Dalcroze Eurythmics and Suzuki systems are wonderful educational approaches which encourage and even integrate voice, movement, percussion, keyboard and other instruments into the teaching of many kinds of music. They're not the problem. What puzzles and concerns me so much is why we cut this valuable integration of the senses out once we become more advanced?

It seems to me that we take away the very qualities, the spontaneous natural disciplines which contribute most to a creative experience—just when we most need them.

So...

Sing what you play, play what you sing, dance what you sing, drum what you dance, drum what you sing—you will open your nervous system, mind, body and spirit to the same creative free flow of energy that inspired Mozart and continues to inspire Jay Greenberg, Rufus Reid, David Darling and Rhiannon.

That's quite a list. Let's make sure to include me and you!

Chapter 3
Finding the Pathway

I have noticed that these three elements—Breath, Pulse and Movement—seem to be present whenever the spirit in music comes alive. By themselves, these elements cannot guarantee that magic will happen; but without these elements, the likelihood of connecting with the spirit in music is significantly reduced. The implication is that we can put together a template based on the ways different performing artists incorporate these elements. And while individual artists will express them differently depending on the styles of music they play and their unique ways of interpreting them, we will finally have a sense of each of the three elements in integration, which will be full of motion, pulse and flow—and be very much alive!

Certainly these elements alone are not enough to create the magic in music. Every performer needs to be free of distractions and to have a clear vision of the musical essence to be communicated. We cannot ignore the need for commitment, trust and relaxed concentration. Even in the most spontaneous improvisations you need some calm and quiet within you to hear the voice of inspiration and respond to its guidance. We also need to be able to translate that guidance into some artistic form of performance.

And with all these foundations in place, there are still no guarantees.

There is just a much better chance of things coming together and our music coming to life.

I use the musical template described briefly above to explore that special aliveness in the performer, to examine its relevance to different kinds of music and levels of performance. Every style of music implies a somewhat different recipe for hosting our process of inspiration. Improvisation is very different from playing Bach or Brubeck, Brazilian salsa or Argentinean tango, yet I firmly believe that the elements of Breath, Pulse and Movement in *all* these kinds of music set the groundwork for that music to come alive.

My *Inner Game of Music* and *Mastery of Music* seminars and bass teaching have given me many opportunities to explore this template, all the way from teaching younger children to the application of these same principles at a more mature level of education in high school and college up to the level of musical professionals and individuals of true genius.

I have been able to work with music teachers in kindergarten through high school and to conduct seminars at universities and conventions for both future and highly trained professional teachers. My daily contacts teaching private bass students from sixth grade through college level have kept me in touch with the application of these principles in private instruction. My Golden Gate Bass Camp has proved to be fertile ground in which to introduce a specific curriculum for young musicians with the participation of an open-minded faculty of colleagues from around the country. And finally, I have been able to work with high school musicians in depth in a variety of public school orchestra, band and choral programs.

These have been the primary models for my experiments, and *Bringing Music to Life* encapsulates what I have learned and taught over a dozen years.

Experimental Workshops: 2005, Inspiration in Music, Oakland, California

The first major test of my theoretical approach of integrating Breath, Pulse and Movement with a mixed group of classical and jazz performers and educators came at my 2005 Inspiration in Music workshop in Oakland, California with an array of brilliant colleagues: improvising cellist David Darling, tai chi master Chungliang Al Huang, vocalist Rhiannon, educator Mary Knysh, and choreographer Alan Scofield.

I already had studied the art of free improvisation with Darling and Music for People (www.musicforpeople.org) for several years, following the principles laid out in Jim Oshinsky's book *Return to Child,* and here was an opportunity to use these methods as part of my template while speaking with jazz and classical singers, folk and classical instrumentalists, and teachers active in the public schools.

I made it very clear to the participants who came to work with these wonderful teachers that my agenda was both to learn how to make music on a more inspirational level and explore the processes or techniques we use and their effectiveness in unleashing the magical qualities in music.

This meant we had to engage in a cross-disciplinary approach. Improvisational singers had to take movement and drumming classes. Classical musicians had to learn to salsa dance. Everyone participated in Scofield's creative daily movement sessions. Teachers had to perform Darling's free improvisations on their clarinets and violins. Knysh led our drum circles in complex vocal and hand patterns. We all learned how to be improvise with "no wrong notes." Everyone had to sing in Rhiannon's vocal circles. And everyone had to learn the Eastern principles of tai chi and find for themselves how they applied to their own forms of expression.

What was most exciting for us all was the impact that crossing over those disciplinary lines so obviously had on our music making—having Rhiannon coach instrumentalists, watching Chungliang Al Huang inspire a string quartet, or Scofield coaching a classical pianist through movement techniques. Something quite extraordinary occurred. It may sound like a paradox, but we found that *the less the teachers knew about the specific techniques their students were trained in, the easier it was for them to reach through and connect with the inspiration in music.*

We shattered the borders between different musical styles, ages, and media. We learned that we are all following the same principles and striving for the same inspiration, even though we speak an enormously wide variety of musical languages. And we found that the most important common element of all was the role of the performer in the transmission of music.

Each one of us has the ability to block or channel inspiration *as it passes through our bodies.*

Our bodies are the vessels of our communication.

When Chungliang Al Huang told us to reach up into the universe and bring the chi energy down through all the parts of our body, mind and spirit, and then send it back out into the universe in one great and inspiring circle of inspiration, we created an environment in which the magic could be present.

It was amazing, profound. I wish my words on this page could transport you there. I would love to introduce you to some of the participants whose work gave me clear glimpses of inspiration moving through voice, pulse and body.

There was Somi Hongo, who came from Japan and registered as a singer, dancer and pianist. I will never forget how during one of our improvisation sessions she overwhelmed our staff and her fellow students with her stunning performance playing—of all things—a chair. When she came onstage, and while other musicians were improvising on their traditional instruments, her whole body seemed to be pulsing with intensity, passion and mystery. Her breathing was visibly building this power as she moved slowly across the stage to the chair, and when she grabbed it, when she moved the chair, she exhaled with an intensity that seemed to amplify the sound of the chair dragging across the stage. I was watching her body language and breathing closely, and just knew she was about to sing from—and when sing she did, her voice was rich with—the same passion her body was pulsing with.

When Miriam Hlavaty, a wonderful classically trained pianist from Norway, improvised in a contemporary style in another session, she too used her body to amplify the intensity of her emotions—but when she played Mozart, her "native" music, it seemed as though she cut herself off from her body and played solely from her intellect or training. This was another opportunity for our extraordinary faculty to coach someone from a different discipline.

In this case, I asked choreographer and movement specialist Alan Scofield to see what he could do to inspire Miriam to use her body more in playing her Mozart sonata. Alan is a brilliant mimic and mine, so he knows what a pianist playing full-bodied, ecstatic Mozart would look like. Alan sat next to Miriam at the piano, and while Miriam played he put his hands above the keyboard and mimed the image of a very physically expressive concert pianist... his hair flying all over the place, his upper body and shoulders swaying, his hips bouncing with the rhythm, his face filled with expressive emotion.

He invited Miriam, who had the piece memorized, to entrain or unite herself with Alan's motions while still playing the notes. It was an astounding theatrical exercise. Miriam threw herself into the part with glee, the music absolutely came to life, and the pair of them brought down the house! It was an utterly convincing testimony to the way the body influences performance, allowing the music to shimmer with energy and excitement!

We were on to something!

I know this sounds all very "California." Many people have come to expect an *anything goes* approach to music making from a part of the world that is known for its liberalism and experimental spirit. But I can assure you that this isn't just to do with Oakland, where I happen to live, or the wonderful San Francisco Bay Area that Oakland is part of—or California! I was working with a wonderfully eclectic variety of musicians from around the world, and this was far from "just a California thing"—this crossing over into musical worlds where people have little or no training or experience, learning to make music come alive!

This workshop invited people to step out of their comfort zones to learn new skills before integrating them with their own familiar instruments or voices. And this crossing over into new territory, where body, mind and spirit, Breath, Pulse and Movement can come together afresh, is the very essence of the change that characterized all our experiments in education.

It takes courage to be willing to do something new with no assurance of success, no knowledge of what the end result might be. It is intimidating to be asked to return to one's childhood, to laugh at oneself, to be passionate or to willing to look foolish— or most important of all, to be quiet, to be still. This approach to music predictably meets with some initial resistance as it pushes and continues to push the comfort zone of our human nature.

But the results! The results justify the approach. That's one thing I am now quite clear about.

The Result Was to Bring Inspiration and Life to Our Music

Did it make a difference? You bet it did!

What was the result? The immediate results, right there in our workshop sessions, were some astonishing, powerful musical performances. Some of the music had so much vitality and depth it brought the performers themselves to tears. Using Darling's *Return to Child* approach, the actual impact of returning to a childhood spontaneity and freedom with all one's musical knowledge and technique intact proved to be extraordinary. It was as though that childhood quality infiltrated our adult performers with a sense of play, spontaneity and enthusiasm they hadn't experienced in years, even decades! There was a fresh spirit in the air that was undeniable, and our excitement became almost addictive, so we'd find ourselves looking for ways to recapture the adrenaline we had experienced in those breakthrough sessions.

Like lightning, inspiration never strikes twice in exactly the same way at exactly the same place; but we were learning to prepare ourselves for the magic, to be open and responsive to it. Several of our participants (myself included!) were inspired to go out after the workshops and take dance lessons, voice and drumming classes! I'm talking professional musicians here, amateurs too, and college-level classical students.

Patricia Miner, an Inspiration in Music participant who is a violinist in several Bay Area regional orchestras, told me the most helpful movement practice she has used to influence her violin playing in this way has been Nia—a new discipline based on the principles of yoga, modern dance and exercise. Prompted by her enthusiasm I have taken some Nia classes myself, and brought Nia teachers to my Bass Camp. Patricia also studied singing and improvisation at the Ali Akbar Khan Institute of North Indian classical music in Marin County, California, and feels that this has helped with her sense of pitch in playing the violin and connecting her breath to her music.

I will return to talk about some more experiences from this workshop in later chapters; here I just want to say that this course launched the interdisciplinary approach that I have since taken on the road to different musical communities, always in search of refinement and further understanding.

Next Stop: VanderCook College of Music, June 2006

While the California experience described above included mostly adult performers of many styles, my experience at VanderCook provided an opportunity to explore how we can share this new approach with public school teachers from kindergarten through high school. VanderCook is one of the leading music teacher training schools and offers a diverse summer curriculum of continuing education offerings for teachers and students taking coursework for advanced degrees.

I was able to design a course that included my popular *Inner Game of Music* and *Mastery of Music* materials, and throw in a little extra stuff as well for a total of over forty hours of contact instruction with a wonderful group of rather traditional Midwestern music educators. I was able to bring Mary Knysh, my colleague from Music for People and Inspiration in Music to supplement my curriculum with improvisation techniques and also hired a local tai chi Master.

Our participants were more than willing to engage in activities like singing, drumming, movement and somewhat childish games as a part of our explorations in the course I called Music Outside the Lines. Even so, presenting these principles clearly enough that they could pass into the public school music classroom would be quite a challenge for our five-day summer course. And while this workshop was a great opportunity to explore inspiration, improvisation, *Inner Game* concentration and the *Mastery of Music* qualities of excellence, in hindsight, I have to admit I wasn't clear enough yet on the methodology for bringing the life-essence of music into the classroom. The concept was percolating, but the coffee wasn't ready.

What this class did offer me was a chance to explore how a group of classroom music teachers would respond to the early stages of a methodology. My *Inner Game of Music* portion remained a classic presentation of these skills of concentration that hasn't really changed over the past two decades of workshops, and this group was as responsive as any I had worked with. The *Mastery of Music* concepts had relevance, too, as an inspirational model leading to further self-assessment and individual development of the qualities of passion, courage, confidence, communication and yes, creativity. The tai chi classes brought a very relevant energy to these adult teachers who were eager use their bodies to move, concentrate and be inspired by teachers far removed from their daily practice of music teaching. And when Knysh introduced any activities that suggested a return to the state of childhood, our participants were eager and willing.

This was a strong clue for me, telling me that everyone in education is really a child at heart—and perhaps one of the reasons people become teachers is to return vicariously to childhood's freedom through their young students. *Hmmmm*, food for thought. This in turn suggested to me that I should stay on this path of intense energy, interest and full participation, looking at the body, the child within and aligning my work with everyone's desire to play without rules and concerns to clutter up the mind.

David Darling's *Sing What You Play and Play What You Sing* technique was another favorite. Knysh led free improvisation exercises, introducing us to melody, groove, solos, duets, accompaniment and ostinato—all with the comforting assurance that there are no wrong notes—and such mottos as *honor the softest sounds, play from silence*, and *silence is your best friend.*

Overall, the challenge of the course was to introduce nontraditional teaching techniques and pedagogy into a curriculum of tests, competitions and ratings and of Fall, Winter and Spring concerts while needing to instruct a classroom of students in how to play all imaginable instruments and sing, and manage to get them to read music fluently and play all the *right* notes, all at the same time!

How in the world could my teaching colleagues find time in a public school schedule to add yet another layer of emphasis on the principles of inspiration I was developing?

I also ran across the feeling that *this just isn't possible in a public school classroom* in Nova Scotia, when the fantastically lively Irish fiddlers and multi-instrumentalist, singing step dancers and pop musicians were performing onstage next to less-advanced and musically challenged middle school bands and anxious, self-conscious choirs of flutes. Something had to change, I was quite clear about that!

At VanderCook, Knysh and I began to hear people saying things like, "I can do this in my class!" We had some music that participants could purchase that included the instrumentalists actually singing or improvising as part of the written score. "Wouldn't it be fun to have a dancer come in and coach my choir? We could sing our parts a lot more than we have been doing." Knysh and I came to the joint conclusion that we weren't so much hoping to introduce new concepts into the classroom as suggesting a change in emphasis toward playfulness, spontaneity, singing, movement and rhythm in the already-packed public school curriculum.

We concluded our course with one major suggestion to these teachers:

> Start with what you feel comfortable with. Do a little of this or a little of that! You don't have to do it every day. Wait for an opportunity to present itself before introducing singing or dancing, or forming a gamelan ensemble with your competition rhythm section! If you look for opportunities, you will find them. Be content at first with being open to the possibilities…

Golden Gate Bass Camp becomes Fertile Ground for Bringing Music to Life!

Just one month later I had an opportunity to carry the principles of Music for People, Inspiration in Music and Music Outside the Lines forward into my own week-long double bass camp with over fifty middle- and high-school bassists, including most of my own private students, a faculty of fourteen teachers, and two additional three-and-a-half-day courses for adults devoted to classical and jazz bass.

It was an opportunity for me to integrate the two hats I wear as a music educator: one as the classically trained bassist and teacher, and the other as the Inner Game guy who's into tai chi and all this other alternative stuff. After three summers of experiments, I can honestly say that I've truly integrated who I am as a bass educator with what I do as an explorer whose grail is to find the elusive magic in music.

For the last nine years our bass course has evolved from my teaching the comprehensive method of my esteemed virtuoso-teacher François Rabbath to a more diverse curriculum that includes fourteen teachers sharing interdisciplinary approaches to music. Over eighty teachers and students come together to jam, scat, move and groove their bodies, voices and beloved basses. This new approach was born out of one particular three-hour session at the 2006 Bass Camp.

Mega-Session: Voice, Rhythm and Movement with Kristin Korb, Pat Klobas, John Clayton and Alan Scofield!

I designed a session that would introduce all eighty-plus bass players onstage to voice, rhythm and movement—and then integrate them as one. This was the template I'd deduced from observing Rufus Reid's jazz-influenced piece and the miraculous free improvs I had experienced participating in David Darling's Music for People.

The class began with a very appropriate Latin/fusion demonstration with jazz bassist Pat Klobas. Pat played a samba and a bossa nova with his colleagues percussionist Curt Moore and vibraphonist Tommy Kessiger. He taught us the three elements that comprised these Latin grooves and we were able to approximate those sounds on the bass. We captured the shaker sound by scratching the bow vertically up and down the strings rather than horizontally. We recreated the sound of the bass drum with the palm of the hand hitting the top of the bass and the clave rhythm by tapping the wood bow on the ebony tailpiece. With an orchestra of sixty bassists we were able to recreate these grooves as a tight ensemble—and it was terrific. Our basses made quite a percussion section!

Step two was to introduce the voice. I asked Kristin Korb, a world-renowned jazz bassist *and* singer, to help our bassists with

Darling's Mantra *Sing What You Play and Play What You Sing*. It is difficult to get our kids to sing—especially the younger middle-school and socially-conscious high-school kids! Yet Kristin was very creative in finding simple ways to trick them into full participation and soon had them belting out vocal sounds that imitated their bass sounds pretty well.

She began with the simple instruction *match the pitch you are playing with your voice*, and then added the idea of sliding up and down a bit. Then we approximated a pizzicato sound with our voices: *boom, boing!* And other sounds had vocal counterparts, too: *pow!* for the bass drum sound we had made by hitting the back of the bass, *pssssssssshhh* for the scratch. Soon we were matching the pitch of our bass, but singing three tones higher! Then holding a note on the bass while singing a brief independent melody. Finally we did a call-and-response. Kristin would sing and play a few notes, and we would sing and play them back.

All of which involved and demanded a lot of levels of voice imitation: percussion sounds, unison pitches, singing, accompaniment with the bass—some pretty complex stuff! But we had crossed over successfully into including our voices in our bass playing while also making a connection between our breathing and inner voice to the outer voice of the bass.

Enter Alan Scofield, my partner for many years in my *Inner Game of Music* work with school orchestras and bands in the Bay Area, who has also taught movement and tai chi classes and dance at our Bass Camp for thirteen years. Now it was time to use Alan's expertise to help us find those parts of our bodies that can move to the spirit in the music. In the case of the Latin music grooves, it is simple enough to look at the actual dances that we are playing, mambo and bossa nova, and see where these sounds connect with our bodies. We learned that the bass drum rhythms worked well with our feet and legs. The next level of shaker rhythms seemed to work best with our shoulders and chest area, sometimes even by moving our necks or rocking our heads. And we could sometimes feel the rippling rhythms of the fastest notes, sometimes eighth or sixteenth notes, in our tongues or even our breathing!

We learned to dance the grooves we played and then we had to find a way to keep that movement alive in our bodies while standing with our basses in our hands! We couldn't move as freely, but we were still alive and grooving, dancing the music in some way. *Wow*! Did this make a difference!

We would play one Latin rhythm with some bassists as percussionists, others singing the percussion rhythms as they played, and *everyone* doing the dance! The sight onstage was completely electrifying and all but out of control! It was totally amazing. The other teachers who were in the hall observing the session started cheering what was happening onstage and screaming! I couldn't believe my ears or my eyes—and everyone was having a total blast!

During this mega-session, our featured jazz clinician was watching and getting ready to take his turn.

Enter John Clayton. John is one of the world's great jazz bassists who has also served as Principal Bassist in the Amsterdam Philharmonic, is an educator and a composer-arranger for many great artists, including Diana Krall. John is an artist with both classical and jazz technique (obviously) and he really integrates all these scat-move-groove elements when he plays his bass. So when he came onstage he concluded the session with more call-and-response grooves while playing and dictating vocal jazz scat sounds.

And while John was leading the ensemble Kristin went around helping people to keep their breath alive and participate with their voices while Alan shouted out parts of the body that can move to the groove. We rocked! There was so much energy loose in that room that by the time we finished everyone was completely fried with exhaustion.

For the next three years Bass Camp continued to provide me with opportunities to explore this integrated approach to learning to play jazz and classical bass. The following year I had Kristin, Alan and myself visit each of the nine smaller ensembles who were performing pieces at our final concert. Each group had a regular bass coach, but the three of us worked only on the vocal, rhythmic and movement possibilities with their music. Our special voice, pulse and movement coaching seems to have brought plenty of humor and life to their final concert. Every one of the groups played with reckless abandon. There were clever movements, some surprise singalongs and overall a level of rhythmic tightness that I had never witnessed at previous camps. They rocked!

In 2006 I introduced a new clinician to Bass Camp. Robert Wallace led a movement-exercise drumming class called Total Rhythm. Robert's classes begin with a carefully crafted tai chi warm-up so no one gets hurt followed by a tremendous musical and physical workout at a relentless tempo. And the participants really are filled with "yea energy." I saw some shy middle-school girls screaming at the top of their lungs and banging on their drums while walking, skipping and performing intricate African call-and-response rhythms—not unlike the rhythms we play on the bass. We needed to bring this kind of energy into our bass classes, and Robert's classes in Total Rhythm certainly unleashed a goodly amount!

The third year of Bass Camp we commissioned two works for our eighty-piece bass orchestra that required players to use their instruments to produce percussion sounds while using their voices and making body movements. Kristin Korb wrote a fabulous piece based on a complex Latin *cascara* rhythm in which the bass groove is built up from the start, much as we had two years earlier. Her score also required the kids to sing along while playing. In 2008 we added a new piece by Donovan Stokes that actually had bassists playing conga drums and bass at the same time.

In addition to Robert Wallace returning, I engaged Curt Moore, another percussionist specializing in Latin and jazz rhythms to coach the *cascara* rhythm in Kristin's large bass orchestra piece. Curt passed out pencils (as drumsticks), brought a drum machine and taught players what it was like to line up interlocking rhythms *perfectly...* not like a bass section, but like percussionists! Curt had us tapping rhythms ranging from a whole note, to half, quarter and eighth notes. Does that sounds simple? It's not so simple when you are talking perfection. Then Curt applied his principles to the intricacies of the *cascara* pattern, and *wow*—what a difference!

This was the proof I needed of the enormous value in training delivered by voice, rhythm and movement experts visiting our classroom. Bringing in outside experts may not always be financially feasible in every educational situation, but there are ways of honoring the value of work that goes beyond the notes and into the world of Breath, Pulse and Movement.

Our movement sessions led by Alan Scofield have an ongoing emphasis on bass music, tai chi, communication games, partnering, dancing to many bass styles (baroque, jazz, Latin, New Age), improvisation, singing and conducting, and I've been collaborating with Alan to find more ways we can use our bodies to communicate our music—but I'll tell you more about that in chapter 6 on movement. That work had its beginnings in this class.

I also engaged a wonderful black belt Nia teacher, Danielle Woermann, to conduct a class designed to integrate music and rhythm with more emphasis on exercise, with music carefully chosen from our bass repertoire. The Nia system is a way of exercising to multicultural music that incorporates elements of tai chi, tae kwon do, aikido, jazz, modern and Duncan dance, and such healing arts as Feldenkrais, Alexander Technique and Yoga. Nia classes turn out to be a fantastic way to connect body and voice with music. The high point of this class came with the group dancing, singing and moving to Bach's lovely *Air on the G String*.

And I continue to add new curriculum elements to Bass Camp. The 2008 Bass Camp introduces new tai chi classes with Emily Rubis and Mary Knysh making her debut teaching free improvisation to bass players in addition to classes in voice and drumming.

The beat goes on!

Applying These Principles to the High School Orchestra

Through the San Francisco Symphony's Education Program I also work with both young bassists and string orchestras in four of the Bay Area's outstanding music programs. This outreach program gave me the opportunity to integrate concepts of Breath, Pulse and Movement into a specially designed and commissioned piece for string orchestra. W. A. Mathieu—an internationally known composer, pianist and theorist, a former professor at the San Francisco Conservatory and Mills College, and a former arranger for jazz greats Stan Kenton and Duke Ellington—was the perfect person to write such a piece.

Heart, Soul and Stomp!

Heart, Soul and Stomp was based on improvisation concepts that I'd learned at David Darling's 2004 Art of Improvisation workshop in collaboration with choreographer Alan Scofield and composer Allaudin Mathieu. The project was funded by the San Francisco

Symphony Education Department under the direction of Ron Gallman, and *Stomp* received its premiere performances by the string ensembles at Acalanes, Campolindo, Lowell High Schools and San Francisco School of the Arts.

Allaudin and I devised a three-movement work that would get high school musicians to express music from the inside out, helping inhibited or self-conscious high school string students to express emotion with their breathing, bodies and instruments, much as we did at our Golden Gate Bass Camp.

Allaudin saw this commission as a way to reconcile what he calls the sad discrepancy between *hot* and *cool* music, which we discussed in chapter 1—*hot* music being the kind that comes directly from your juices without need of notation, and *cool* music being the kind that's carefully composed and scored by a composer and then played as written.

Both ways of making music have their advantages and their share of geniuses, and I myself love both ways and have spent a lifetime looking for recipes for compromise and accommodation. *Heart, Soul and Stomp* is an attempt to introduce reading musicians to both aspects at once—making considerable demands on them at both extremes—building a direct emotional connection in the moment while reading difficult ensemble music from the page.

We composed the piece with sections for shy, mostly Asian students, for uninhibited "out-of-control" performing arts school students and for cool, affluent students from the East Bay. Each school was given the same musical score to learn and internalize and then spontaneously recreate with total abandon! High school students wouldn't usually play conventional notes printed on the page with that kind of free-wheeling spirit, but when we wrote *acting frustrated, stomping, singing* and *hip hop moves* in the music, and with the help of enthusiastic conductors, choreographer specialist

Alan Scofield, the composer W. A. Mathieu and my own relentless supervision at most of the rehearsals, the kids just had no choice!

The piece begins with string players making vocal sounds that express anxiety, relief, excitement, laughter, sarcasm, frenzy and the cooing of a baby in its crib, and then finding the same sounds on their string instruments. They were required to create vocal sounds that imitated the feelings they were playing on their instruments, i.e., laughter. Remember David's Music for People mantra? *Sing What You Play and Play What You Sing*. They also had to sing some of the melodic lines they were simultaneously playing on their string instruments. What a beautiful sound that was!

Acalanes High School freshman violinist Helen Wang told me that when she first played the piece, she thought it was "bizarre, insane and weird."

> When we play Baroque or Classical music, we are taught not to have feelings but just to play the right notes, dynamics and fingerings. The idea of making the music our own by expressing our own emotional feelings was really new to us. Most of us are just not comfortable putting ourselves out there and sticking out in the group. But when I was sitting in the back of the section, surrounded by friends, I found I was comfortable goofing off and not taking the music so seriously so I had fun dancing to the hip-hop groove— and then when Mr. Green used dancing and playing as an example, we all started to really get involved—we really liked it!"

The "Heart" movement is all about feelings. Jerry Panone, the director from the School of the Arts wrote:

The music was always interesting and challenging, especially the extra-musical requirements of the piece, since the students had to leave their familiar comfort zone of simply playing their instruments. The requirements of breathing and vocalizing as well as imitating emotions and feelings on their instruments was especially helpful in connecting students with the essence of phrasing, and the emotional experience of playing the music behind the notes.

Example 3.1. *Heart, Soul, & Stomp,* movement 1: "Heart," W. A. Mathieu

The "Soul" movement contained more lyrical writing, with some breathlessly beautiful harmonies. Allaudin described his inspiration for this movement this way:

> For the Soul movement, I went back to my own teenage years and felt the longing and loneliness and ecstasy of those years. This is the movement I would have written at that time if I'd had the chops.

And the final movement, "Stomp," was based on a hip-hop groove and included kids stomping on different beats while dancing in their seats. The kids really rocked it with "Stomp!"

Allaudin commented,

> This was where we were trying to teach the kids something they already knew internally, but with the cognitive complexity of musical notation—really getting at both sides of the hot music/cool music paradox!

Example 3.2. Heart, Soul & Stomp, movement 3: "Stomp," W. A. Mathieu

Alan Scofield got the students to overcome their inhibitions and play with reckless abandon! He told me later:

> Their sound was very good, but there was more inside them, more in their bodies waiting and wanting to come out. I urged them to dance with their upper bodies (like Helen Wang!) and to rock in their chairs while stomping on the designated beats. I'm sure they thought I was mad…

The four performances were memorable concert experiences for both audiences and students. In every single performance the music making was spontaneous, theatrical, engaging, humorous, beautiful and exciting, and the crowds were on the edges of their seats! I fervently believe the reason this piece was such a success (besides being a brilliantly crafted piece of music) was that the students *had* to be engaged with their voices, feelings, bodies and energy in order to play it.

The Eyes Have It

I also believe we hear a lot of music with our eyes. It sounds a bit strange to say it that way, of course, but when we see students in performance staring at their music, fingers and bows and not, repeat *not,* engaging their bodies, this transmits boredom and doubt to the those of us in the audience and invites us to become less engaged with the music—and more critical. On the other hand, when we see movement, life and spirit onstage we get caught up in the energy and are more receptive to its spirit. So we're hoping that the connections our students began to form in this piece will develop and deepen over the course of their musical lives.

Michele Winter, the director at San Francisco's Lowell High School said:

I'm convinced that having made the connection between heart, soul, mind, body, and music in this piece, my students will be looking for similar connections in every piece they play.

That's certainly what we're hoping.

Harvey Benstein, the director of the Campolindo orchestra, told me,

The *Heart, Soul and Stomp!* project was a terrific experience that captivated my students and allowed them to get totally into the music, leaving the majority of their inhibitions behind. The project allowed performers to return to their basic love of music making, similar to their earliest experiences with music and creating sounds on their instrument.

Harvey's comment reminds me of one of Music for People's publications which I've mentioned before: *Return to Child,* the MFP manual by Jim Oshinsky.

The life and spirit in music has always been present with our children as they play and dance with their bodies, sing spontaneously and groove to the rhythms of the music, and the same spirit can be found in every piece of music we play in classical, folk, jazz, chamber or large ensemble music. Our challenge as teachers is to find ways to trick our students into *returning to their childlike playfulness* with Mozart, Brubeck and Metallica.

We created this experience for these orchestral kids by writing in the singing, acting and rhythmic moving as parts of the musical score. Now that they have had this experience it is up to their teachers to remind the kids where these same elements of rhythm and excitement are present in the music of other composers such as Tchaikovsky. Music must come *through* our bodies, heart and soul. It cannot communicate itself from the printed page via the brain and out through the fingers *without* being felt and internalized *from the inside out.*

I cannot overstate the profound impact these four performances had on the audiences at all four spring concerts. Not only had the music come alive through these students' performance with their acting, singing, grooving and incredible playing, but the attention from the audience was completely engaging. No one in any one of those concert halls could miss the fact that this music jumped right off the stage and had an energy and life that moved everyone in attendance—and the kids had a terrific time playing the piece as well.

And *Heart, Soul and Stomp!* is now available from the composer, who can be contacted through his website at www.coldmountainmusic. com or via e-mail at info@coldmountainmusic.com—so you can hear it and see what I mean!

My Second Year with the Heart, Soul and Stomp Schools

My next challenge was to maintain this same level of experience with these kids while applying the same principles to music that was *not* written by for them by W. A. Mathieu.

The Bass Camp experience has taught me that you cannot do everything all in one year: it has to come in stages. So the next stage was to incorporate some of the specialty visits we'd enjoyed at Bass Camp with voice specialist Kristin Korb, movement specialist Alan Scofield and rhythm guru Curt Moore.

The plan for 2007–08 was to have each of these specialists twice as well as several visits in which I would be integrating Breath, Pulse and Movement. I planned to use YouTube clips of jazz singers, pianists, Latin groups, chamber groups, string quartets, orchestras, conductors, rap and hip-hop bands to show the kids how these artists use their breath in different ways and how they can do this themselves with their own music. We also planned to take rhythm exercises from a passage in Tchaikovsky's *Fourth Symphony* to show that we are all really percussionists—but percussionists using notes and bows and voices instead of sticks or mallets. Each of our guest teachers would visit the school and give an introductory session in their specialty, and in their second visit they would literally show these students where they are doing the same things in the music they are playing in their upcoming concert.

The beauty of this program is that the fabulous conductors in these schools have carried forward these lessons with their orchestras and bands in our absence. When I returned to Lowell, Michele showed me how students are now singing and can move with their instruments and breath. At Campolindo High School, Harvey Benstein has his kids doing movement exercises and transcribing percussion rhythms by playing *col legno battuto* (hitting the strings with the wood of their bow rather than playing sustained notes with the hair side), and Jerry Panone has been confronting his kids to get out of their macho self-images and into the character of the music they play.

We are well on our way to integrating this pedagogical approach into these school music programs and actually creating a new norm that aims to bring out the spirit in the music along with all the correct notes and rhythms. In the spring of 2008 the Lowell High School orchestra presented *Heart, Soul and Stomp!* at the California State Music Educator's Convention—and I will continue to introduce these concepts through articles in educational journals and at many conventions around the country.

An Ongoing Invitation

If you're a music educator, please consider this chapter as an invitation to see how you can assimilate this new pedagogical approach into the teaching you have already been doing with enthusiasm and success for some time.

The challenge here is balance and integration: how can you take these skills that are already present in everything we experience in music and perhaps shift the emphasis in ways that allows more magic in actual performance? Can we add a new goal to our teaching, one that specifically includes bringing life and spirit to the music we make?

My suggestion is that we should go deeper into our understanding and experience of the three core elements of Breath, Pulse and Movement, and that as our conscious enrichment in these areas proceeds, more life and spirit will naturally emerge in our performances.

In Part II we will go deeper into these skills and explore some new pathways that present themselves along the way.

Let's go make music!

Part II
The Three Techniques

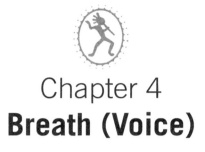

Chapter 4
Breath (Voice)

When we sing without words, first just following the breath, then
the sound of a sigh, and then the song, our journey leads us with
the energy of emotion into a place of clarity and integration; a
reunion with our true nature.

—Susan Osborne

Breath Comes from the Air

Breath is the energy of our inspiration.

Kokomon Clottey is a marvelous African drummer, educator
and peacemaker, and the author of *Beyond Fear* and *Mindful
Drumming*. Kokomon once told me that the universe can be
reduced to just two elements: Air and Pulse—and coming from
such a master of complex rhythms, I was struck by the beautiful
simplicity of this way of seeing things. He went on to tell me that
if we are to translate these two elements into art, we must first
take that air into our bodies in the form of breath. So the universe
provides us with the air, we humans embrace this air and bring it
into our bodies, and as we expel the air, the process is transformed
into our art.

From air, via breath, to music…

Don Campbell, author of *The Mozart Effect, Creating Inner
Harmony,* and many other books on the voice likes to trace things

musical back to their origins in the breath, too. He told me:

> The human impetus to make sound is fundamental for life. What causes a child's initial impulse to coo? What's the instinct that makes us want to sound out the beginning of an Aa or Ee or Oooo... before it becomes a note, before it has any rhythm? We make these sounds before art enters our lives.
>
> I love it that the voice makes an imprint on the breath which gives us individuality from the moment we are born. It embosses our breath with personality as well as information. It is the way a baby says I am.

In Campbell's audio tape series, *The Healing Power of Chant*, the sound of monks chanting closely resembles the sounds an infant hears in the womb before it comes into this world. The impulse to make sound is truly a universal language, and ancient chants can connect us to the primal sounds of our birth and the language of life itself.

Susan Osborne, a great singer, healer and educator tells us,

> Singing is the direct language of the soul. It is a universally understood means of communication, going beyond words, from one body to another. And it is freely available to everyone regardless of talent.

We can think of singing, then, as a part of this chain of experience that begins with the air and then breath. When we sing, we are *vibrating* the exhaling of our breath.

I am jealous of singers of all kinds, I must admit. As a bassist I have to say I envy the fact that the singer's instrument, the voice, is right there within the body, and that the form of self-expression is so direct and immediate. Singers can be inspiring models for other instrumental artists because they have such a natural and immediate connection to their music, to the message their songs convey and to the inspiration which they must transmit to their audience.

Ethnic music from cultures around the world, whether it be North- or South-Indian classical, African, Chinese or Balinese, contain notes and scales that are quite different from the major and minor scales used in European classical music. In non-Western cultures, too, music is often inseparable from some form of spiritual practice, as with the Indian system of ragas, or, as in African music, where it can be an integral part of a cultural tradition of drumming, dancing and singing which is itself inseparably linked to the community with its hunting, life rituals, tales of heroic ancestors, healing ceremonies and worship.

In his book *Music: Physician for Times to Come*, Don Campbell explores the human voice and chanting as forms of physical therapy, psychotherapy and spiritual practice. I will limit the scope of our journey here to the basic uses of the breath as it relates to our inner and outer voices and its ultimate application to the performance of music, but I invite you to follow any pathways in sound, tone or voice study that you feel will deepen your ability to use your breath in making music.

Many great artists like Yo Yo-Ma, Bobby McFerrin and Paul Winter have spent years living, studying and playing with musicians in Asia, South America, Brazil, Spain, Africa and Indonesia, and their experiences have brought a wonderful and new global sound to our Western styles of jazz, fusion, rock, folk and contemporary classical music.

I hope you will feel inspired to look into any of these multicultural roads that catch your interest, and I can assure you that as an artist you will find that these other forms of music can enrich your life and influence your musical performance. You are likely to become a better musician while learning overtone singing, or studying Indian ragas, and I encourage you to explore different musical cultures as a part of your musical development.

I find it fascinating that each and every one of these styles of music will likely connect you to your breath and your voice—because breath and voice are our most direct path to inspiration.

Watch Great Artists and Learn from Them

I first got excited about learning to use my voice when I was participating in vocal warm-ups during David Darling's Music for People. I already knew it was important to breathe through my mouth (and not to hold my breath) while I played my bass, and I knew the value of being able to sing what I played and then play what I sang. But I had never worked on my voice as a part of my bass playing. Connecting with my breath *while* I was actually playing just wasn't part of the way I was taught to play the bass.

Then David showed me how to open up the connection between my breath, voice, and bass—and my inspiration.

He used simple exercises like call-and-response, singing over a drone, vocalizing to simple tai chi movements, babbling, making ambulance siren sounds and eventually singing the pitches I was playing—you can take a look at the Music for People manual *Return to Child* for the basic concepts, or listen to *The Darling Conversations* (available at www.musicforpeople.org). And after we'd been through these initial exercises, he taught me to harmonize by singing along while playing the bass.

Darling's improvisation courses are held on the East Coast and I live in the San Francisco Bay Area on the West Coast. So when he saw how inspired and keen I was becoming to do more work with my voice, he encouraged me to connect up with a man he considered one of the greatest musicians in the world: William Allaudin Mathieu.

Allaudin Mathieu is a master of both Eastern and Western music. He is a disciple of the great North Indian vocalist Pandit Pran Nath and the master musician Hamza El Din. He is a master of overtone singing and a fluent scholar, composer and performer in both Eastern and Western styles as well as the author of *The Harmonic Experience* and *The Listening Book*.

Allaudin pointed out that much of our musical experience has to do with being *in tune* or *in resonance* with something. On some level, everything is connected, and we are always in relationship. It is our nature to be connected, to be in *unison* with something, to *resonate* with aspects of our environment. We are not much used to thinking in these terms, but the truths they express are very basic. These are powerful concepts and they directly relate to why it is so much *fun* to play with others, to play or dance in synch with others, to be in tune.

Singing in Tune: It's about Resonance

Allaudin points out that people like to join together in community. This is why string players feel a kinship with other string players, and singers with other singers. But there is another kind of resonance that is based directly on vibration. Allaudin reminded me that two bass strings tuned to the same pitch but physically separate from one another can make each other vibrate through what is known as sympathetic vibration.

When one string is in tune with the other, it will resonate. That's just the nature of waves, it's how the universe is put together: you could call it acoustic-harmonic synchronicity.

And when we as musicians have never been taught to sing in tune, we will naturally be missing something in our understanding of resonance.

Allaudin himself told me how moved and impressed he was when he first heard the terrific trombone sounds of the Stan Kenton Band; later he would compose for both Stan Kenton and Duke Ellington. At first he didn't know what made the trombone section of these bands produce such great music—music with so much harmonic resonance. He told me,

> At the time, I didn't know what in tune meant. And then, when I heard Ravi Shankar for the first time, I had a breakthrough experience: I realized there is something in Shankar's music that sounds just like Stan Kenton's trombone section—the sound I think is so terrific, but just don't understand. It took me a while to put the two experiences together.

> I studied some Indian music, and learned to sing the first pitches of the scale in tune. I listened for the first time in my life to the simple effect of two notes, one in relationship to the other. And I noticed that whether the notes were in tune or out of tune had enormous psychological impact. Resonance was the key! So I was able to learn raga by studying the relationship between two notes. I became these frequencies, these resonances. Your voice is set up to explore and exploit these relationships.

There is something very powerful and profound about this concept of resonance, the idea of being in relationship with, or perfectly in tune with, another pitch. Resonance is what connects all the musicians in an ensemble and opens us to inspiration so the music we make has energy and vitality. I have come to believe that we all have a basic desire to be *in community* with those we can find a *resonance* with, a drive to be, quite literally as well as metaphorically, in *harmonic relationships*—and that this is one of the main reasons we participate in music making.

Activity: Singing in Tune

Let's get started. Focus on the simplest things. Let's experience this phenomenon of *singing in tune*, and see how it affects the spirit of our music.

1. You can play a single string on a guitar or any stringed instrument, but don't use a piano.
   a. An electronic keyboard will do if you use the flute or clarinet setting, or you can sing in tune with a friend of the same gender and at the same pitch.
   b. Concentrate on singing just the same notes.
2. Take a deep breath and match your partner's (or the keyboard/string instrument's) pitch.
3. Now sing a different pitch (any pitch) while your partner/ instrument holds the original pitch, thus creating a musical interval of two pitches.

Reflection

1. What did it feel like when you sang perfectly in tune?
2. Could you hear your voice when it was in a perfect unison or did it disappear?

3. What kind of vibration or resonance did you feel between your voice and the tone of the string (or the other person)?
4. How did it feel when you were singing unison as compared to other intervals?

Allaudin talks about being in communion with the universe by being in unison with one string, one pitch, one person. Music is a way we can entrain with others, coming into resonance with them. He explains,

> Some theologians and metaphysicians may be able to look at the big picture and somehow translate that down into everyday life, but let me tell you, I go at it the opposite way. I found out what the universe was about by first finding out what unison is, musically, and only then did I realize that what I was exploring was the very fabric of the universe!

> I woke up to the essence of music a little late, I'm afraid. I always understood how beautiful music was, but I didn't really understand why until I was in my late twenties—and then I began to see that the whole point wasn't to write atonal scores and impress the academics, but to sing a note in tune and see what happens! And when I sing a tonic in tune with my teacher, what happens is truly something special!

One of the reasons we hear more about the spiritual connection in vocal rather than instrumental music has to do with the physical engagement that's involved: the physical connection through the vibration of the voice to the nervous system, the ear and sense of balance, and to states of well-being.

Studies published as early as 1830 have shown that music evokes physiological responses and affects blood pressure. The research of the French physician, psychologist and ear specialist Alfred Tomatis shows that vibrations pass through our skin, bones and ears to stimulate electrical impulses to the brain which promote physical health and balance: if the body doesn't experience sound and vibration, it will decay.

The monks at a French monastery became listless and fatigued after the Second Vatican Council and a new abbot "revised" their activities to eliminate chanting from their daily routine. When Tomatis was called in, he told the monks that the sound and vibration of their chanting had physically charged their nervous systems and recommended they start chanting again if they wanted to return to their previous state of high energy and good health. His cure worked.

Graham Welch, Director of Educational Research at the University of Surrey in the United Kingdom, wrote:

> People who sing are healthier than people who don't. Singing gives the lungs a workout, tones abdominal and intercostal muscles and the diaphragm, and stimulates circulation. It makes us breathe more deeply than many forms of strenuous exercise, so we take in more oxygen, improve aerobic capacity and experience a release of muscle tension as well.

I always feel inspired, stronger and healthier when I walk along by the ocean and hear the crashing of ocean waves, and the sound of the ocean reminds me of the sound of my breath, or even the human voice. Humans generally hear sound waves whose frequencies are between 20 and 20,000 Hz, and ocean waves contain the same full spectrum of vibrations. When I listen to recordings of Benedictine monks chanting, that too reminds me of the sound of ocean waves with its full range of acoustic stimulation, and this suggests another connection—one with the physical release of the brain chemical serotonin that accompanies the feeling of well-being and physical balance. It is this complete harmonic and acoustic resonance that we feel throughout the body which gives us the sense of being alive and in relationship with the world around us.

Chanting can also be a powerful tool for developing clarity of mind. The Indian teacher Swami Muktananda wrote,

> Chanting is a significant and mysterious practice. It is the highest nectar, a tonic that fully nourishes our inner being. Chanting opens the heart and makes love flow within us. It releases such intoxicating inner bliss and enthusiastic splendor, that simply through the nectar it generates, we can enter the abode of the Self."

Don Campbell points out that chanting differs in important ways from the traditional way we sing hymns in the West. Chant is based on an elongation of the physical breath while singing notes which stay within a close melodic range of five or six tones. By incorporating deep, slow breathing, it facilitates a state of contemplative listening and calm serenity while realigning brain, heart and breath.

Sylvia Nakkach is a distinguished voice educator, scholar and singer who conducts many courses which explore and demonstrate the benefits of singing. Her exercises and articles are published on her website (www.voxmundiproject.com). Here are two of her exercises from the Vox Mundi Project:

Activity: Chanting and Toning

1. Stand up or sit with
   a. your hands free of tension,
   b. chin parallel to the floor,
   c, eyes softly focused, neither closed nor completely open.
2. Take a deep breath, keeping the shoulders down.
   a. Bring your open hands and arms near your belly
   b. while holding the breath in the pelvic cavity for few seconds.
3. Exhale slowly, directing the air upward toward your crown.
4. Release your hands and arms.
5. Repeat at least three times.
6. Find a recording of Benedictine monks performing Gregorian chant and sing along!

Activity: Vocal Release— an Effortless Voice Practice

1. Allow sound to follow breath and voice to follow sound.
2. Release a vocal tone like "wuu" through a small, relaxed lip opening, as if you were humming.
3. Sustain your focus on that specific tone, toning (singing to simple vowels, *Ahh, Eee, Ohh, Ouu,* while sustaining your pitch) over a subtle drone played by an external instrument or device.
4. Keep a clear sense of sounding one note and dwelling in that tonal space.

Feeling and Singing

Vibration focuses us in on feeling.

Allaudin says that we don't know quite how this works. There is a mystery to harmony, and it has to do with the tonal aspects of music, the experiences we have when we're singing in tune at a perfect fifth or in unison, or playing a string instrument held against the body. These things are highly affecting and give us a feel for the ebb and flow of the music.

In earlier centuries there was a theory which described certain intervals as sad or happy, or expressive of longing, jealousy or rage. In Plato's time it was forbidden to sing tunes in the Dorian mode to soldiers because the feeling associated with that modal scale was thought to encourage lethargy. Maybe so, maybe not. Bach wrote a marvelous toccata in the Dorian mode, and it's far from lethargic. Perhaps it is best not to believe what others tell you about the way music feels. But you can feel it, and you can describe it for yourself.

Allaudin says,

> We know that an interval such as a minor third may have an effect of sadness on most listeners, at least in our culture, but in other cultures this same interval can have quite a different feeling and meaning. Within Western harmony and culture, we can often agree on the meaning and feelings implied in music, but in reality, there are no feelings *in* the music. It is our response to music that brings up these feelings within each one of us. We certainly know how two people can hear the same political speech and a Republican will have one response while a Democrat might have quite a different reaction—and the same can be true of music.

If the performer experiences a feeling strongly and communicates it through the breath, pulse and body with intensity and integrity, it stands a very good chance of affecting the audience. So in essence, it isn't really the notes that are being delivered but the mode and *feeling* of the delivery that matters. In terms of our communications when we're talking among friends, too, our tone of voice may be more important than the actual words we choose.

Activity: Communicating Feeling

1. Think of something very calm and peaceful—a lake, a scene in nature—your choice.
2. Take a deep breath and *inhale* this feeling.
3. As you exhale, say the sound *Ahhhh* in the spirit of the peace you are feeling. The peacefulness is in the breath.
4, Repeat steps 1–3 with a feeling of anger or rage. *Inhale* the feeling of anger and exhale it as loud as you dare with the sound *Aaaaaa!*
5. Repeat steps 1–3 with a feeling of anxiety or nerves. *Inhale* your fear and *exhale* the sound *Aaaayeeee!*

Reflection

1. When you inhaled, when did the breath transform into a feeling?
2. Was this a simple thing to do?
3. How did you feel when your inhaled feelings matched the exhaled feelings?

Activity: Feeling One Thing and Communicating Another

1. Think of something very calm and peaceful.
2. Inhale and exhale the feeling of peacefulness *while expressing anxiety in your voice with the sound* Aaahhhhhh!

Reflection

1. Can you describe any feelings of conflict when you are feeling peaceful and expressing anxiety at the same time?
2. If so, perhaps you will agree that it is difficult to feel one thing (say, nervousness) and express calmness in your performance at the same time.

The lesson here is that feelings come into the body as we breathe in and the air enters our lungs, and leaves transformed into a state of consciousness or feeling.

The music we make follows a similar path of transformation. It starts with air which is then translated into breath. Breath in turn is transformed into resonance or vibration. We experience this vibration within the body. This in turn may pass through our fingers as they touch an instrument, through our lips as we buzz a mouthpiece or reed, or even through the vocal chords as they vibrate within the throat. Since our voice or body can resonate with the breath through the flow of air or unison singing, it offers us the closest possible connection to our actual feelings.

And the closer we can stay with this resonance the more effective we can be in passing it along in the music.

How Indian Ragas Connect Us with Feelings in Music

The study of Indian music can be a lifetime spiritual practice, and a great many outstanding jazz, folk and classical artists have been inspired to study Indian classical music as a way of unlocking emotional and spiritual connections. I, too, have been fascinated and moved by its long history and the traditions that centuries of Indian scholars and performers have followed and codified. This kind of music offers another testimony to the connection between performer and inspiration.

Since Allaudin lives and works so comfortably in both worlds simultaneously, I asked him to explain why Indian music is so often associated with spirituality and enlightenment. Once again he brings us back to the idea of vocal resonance that is the foundation of Indian music.

Indian music is sung and played in what is called just intonation. This is a very different style of tuning from our western equal temperament system. Just intonation refers to a system of tones that are in simple prime frequency relationship to the generating tone and to each other. If you study it properly, just intonation will give you a prolonged, practical and highly applicable experience with states of resonance, which will be greatly to your benefit in the classical world, too.

That's why so many musicians gravitate towards Indian music. And the system has been explored over many centuries, so that it now has great detail and structure. Everything is named and identified, just as it is in mathematics. You start with a simple tone and build it up.

For me, the modes have become a way of life—they are the *gods* I live with. They are states of being.

Western, equal temperament music achieves its goal in a different way. I'd say that equal temperament isn't exactly opposed to just intonation—but they may have a somewhat stormy marriage!

East or West—Maybe You Don't Have to Choose...

Don Campbell has lived in many cultures and studied their chanting, ragas and instrumental music, both in the East and the West. While different musical cultures have different approaches, they also have similar functions. Don believes that the simple exercise of toning (singing and sustaining pitches to simple vowels such as *Ahh, Eee, Ohh, Ouu*) can be a bridge between East and West:

> Eastern scales and ragas are still alien to many in the west. We are all familiar with Do Re Me—but we don't have to choose. Just do what works for you! Make up any sound to match the natural flow in the voice, whether it's modal, or the simple do-re-mi. Go into the sound. Just *humm*. Then bring in the body, improvisation, and movement. Once the impetus gets going, there *are* no rules—just structure. And teachers can design exercises that help the voice find freedom.
>
> Sing along, echo, harmonize, resonate, speak—all these wonderful things can develop into rich vocal performance. The Ahh, Eee, Ohh, and Ouu each have their own flavors, emotions, and feelings...

Techniques for Using Breath and Voice

As Kokomon Clottey pointed out so simply and eloquently, air is the source of inspiration. It is transformed into our inhaled breath, and thus into a vibration that we ultimately transmit as feeling into sound.

There are several ways musicians can integrate their breath in their music.

Arriving at Unison

The singer's voice is already located within the body, and for those who play wind instruments, their breath is already part of the sound they create. But I want to distinguish between the voice we hear in our heads (not physically vibrating) and the voice that is in our throats, and to note the aspect of resonance within the body and that part which is outside the body, in the instruments we play. Our goal here is for the inner (mental, non-vibrating) and outer (throat, body and instrumental) resonances to merge in unison.

The thing is to bring the various voices into alignment. If we sing in tune with a single note played on the guitar, violin or bass, we have *two* external sounds: the voice and the string. And similarly, singers can bring their external voice (in the throat) in tune with the internal voice (in the head). We can even bring the external sound of our string or wind instrument in tune with the internal voice in our head.

The idea is to bring about an experience of voices in unison.

Watching Jazz Musicians as They Sing Along

Clips of almost any famous musician are available at YouTube (www.youtube.com/). Check out the great jazz pianist Oscar Petersen, or one of my favorite bass players like John Clayton, Kristin Korb or the late Ray Brown. Watch the great conductor Leonard Bernstein, or pianist Emanuel Ax.

Study these musicians closely and notice their mouths as they perform. You will see several ways that these artists use their breath while they are playing or conducting. Most of the time you will notice their mouths are open and they are breathing freely.

Watch Oscar Petersen playing piano while he is just flat-out enjoying the music. You may see his mouth or lower lip moving to the rhythm of the melody. Now listen carefully, and you may hear him begin to *groan*! That's right, he could be groaning along, making no effort to match the pitch, but still in rhythm with the music. It may sound pretty awful to you. Or you might notice a performer finally begins to sing along with the notes they are playing—singing scat.

Sometimes a pianist or bassist will vocalize a different aspect of the music. Perhaps they sing the rhythm while playing the melody. A conductor might vocalize the violin part while indicating the rhythm that's played by the percussion section. And my dear friend David Darling often sings to his own accompaniment or uses his voice as an instrument to provide rhythmic texture or add extra notes to a chord.

Now that you have had a chance to observe these different uses of the breath and voice, let's experiment with this exercise:

Activity: Sing Along with Your Playing

Find a guitar, string instrument, or keyboard. You need to play three notes for this exercise: do-re-mi, or C–D–E.

1. Play these pitches as quarter notes on an instrument, repeating each note four times: C–C–C–C–D–D–D–D–E–E–E–E.

2. Breathe naturally through your mouth while playing these pitches.

3. Continue playing these notes, now grunting or groaning with each pitch as you play it.

4. Repeat these twelve notes (do-re-mi times four) and sing them as you play them, matching \pitch and rhythm with your voice.

5. Now *sustain* the C (or do) for four beats on the instrument, but *vocalize* over that pitch four repeated C's, singing a rhythmic pattern over a long, sustained pitch.

6. There are some variations on this exercise which get a little more complex and difficult:

   a. Sustain the C on the instrument while you sing the three pitches do-re-mi in any order as often as you like.

   b. Improvise with your voice…just let anything come out.

Example 4.1

Reflection

1. How did you feel when you just groaned or sang the same pitches?
2. What did you notice when you sang a different rhythm from the one you were playing on your instrument?
3. How did it feel when you sang something that was independent of the notes you were playing?

Connecting Your Body with Your Voice

Someone who had been observing me playing my bass once came up to me and asked me,

How can you possibly play that bass without any frets or marks on your fingerboard? How can you find those notes?

I thought for a moment, then answered her question by asking her a question of my own: "Can you sing *Mary Had a Little Lamb* for me?"

It turned out that she was able to do this without thinking, and her song came out perfectly in tune. So I asked her another question: "How did you do that without any frets in your throat!?"

At first she was a little confused, but then she realized that it was possible because she *knows the tune*! I invited her to think of my bass strings as though they were like the "strings" in her throat. I'm able to connect with these strings as if they are part of my body even though they are located outside it.

We humans have this incredible ability to transfer what is in the mind into the body, and even project it beyond the body, where it can reach other people. Think of the way a quarterback can throw a football fifty yards spiraling down the field and have it land on the outstretched fingertips of a sprinting receiver! It's almost unbelievable!

How can a bass player think of one precise pitch on an instrument that has a string forty-two inches long, and then place a hand on the instrument with his eyes closed and hit the exact spot perfectly in tune? It may seem miraculous, and perhaps it is. But it is possible. And it is possible because we have projected our mind out into the world around us and connected with that string!

It may take years of practice before we can place a finger onto a string and have it reflect the precise pitch in our imagination. Without the inner voice controlling the outer voice it would be impossible. But when the action is connected to its source in our inner voice, it is, indeed, possible!

This suggests that the control of our voice or any instrument comes from inside our bodies! We must first have a voice in our head that sings or makes sounds, and then we can imitate or sing along with this inside voice outside our bodies with a second set of resonators that could be our vocal cords, a string instrument, a wind instrument or even a piano.

The challenge for musicians is to match the music we're making outside with the voice in our heads and to maintain a clean connection moment by moment between the two. Perhaps you can hear a song in your head that is perfectly in tune but are unable to sing or play it in tune. This is a case where the body isn't precisely following the voice. Once again, our aim is to achieve a state of perfect resonance between the inner and outer voices, and when they become one it's a thrill! That is why it is so important for us to be *able to match* a *pitch perfectly in unison or in tune.*

The principle of resonance suggests that we want to join in and be together, not only with ourselves but with anyone else we might play with in a small group or large orchestra, so the resonance we've been talking about between internal and external voices can be extended to include many voices.

Singing Louder Inside

In *The Listening Book,* Allaudin Mathieu talks about how important it is to sing what we are playing, but he also makes a particular point here—and I felt I had to put this wonderful lesson to work right away while I was reading his book! Mathieu says that your inner voice must sing *louder* than your outer voice! That way, the "good" music that you know and love and can play freely in your imagination can dominate the sound that you create with your instrument.

What an interesting concept! And it makes perfect sense, because if you sing softly with your inner voice and your outer voice drowns it out, you won't be able to adjust your playing and match the proper pitch. It's like having your teacher play or sing along with you in unison, but they play or sing a little louder than you so that you can shadow their pitches. One voice has to take the lead, the other follow. And we want the leader to be the *inner voice*, because that's the one which plays perfectly in tune and with style.

I recently performed a very difficult bass concerto written by the New York Philharmonic's composer/bassist Jon Deak with the Duluth Symphony Orchestra. Jon's music is contemporary, but still based on western harmony and with very appealing melodies. But while his harmonies are traditional, Jon frequently changes key signatures. As a result, it's critical to play his pieces precisely in tune or they sound very wrong!

This concerto was based on the story of *Jack and the Beanstalk,* and I struggled for a while with one very difficult melodic passage that represents Jack climbing the beanstalk. The rehearsal on the last day before the concert did not go well. I was not playing with perfect intonation; in fact, I was really struggling with this passage. I knew I had only one more rehearsal the next morning to get the passage right, and it had reached the point where I was even considering cutting it. But then I and everyone else would know I had given up—that the music was difficult and I wasn't good enough to play it!

Which would have been very embarrassing indeed.

I went back to my room. I knew I had to do something different to allow me to play more in tune. And then I remembered Allaudin explaining that the voice inside my head needed to be *louder* than the voice of my bass.

I sat down with the bass part and began to not only *think* the music in my head but to *sing* this difficult passage out loud. If I could sing this section of this piece in tune and *louder* than I play my bass—which meant belting it out loud in my Holiday Inn room while a whole bunch of out-of-town musicians were sleeping nearby!

I could immediately *feel* the difference! Yes, I knew the melody in my head. And I knew when I was out of tune that something was wrong. But now my inner voice (both in my head, and resonating *with* my vocal cords) was in control and dominating what my bass was doing. And yes, I was drowning out my bass playing with my singing along! I sang that passage over and over and couldn't get it *out* of my head.

The next morning at the rehearsal, I gave my external voice a rest but let my inner voice rip—and let my bass follow along. And she played it perfectly. *Wow*…what a lesson!

What I didn't realize was that my bass had been badly damaged during the flight from California to Minnesota. With a wonderful rehearsal under my belt, I felt I was all ready and prepared for my performance—but I was about to get the surprise of my life.

During my flight, my bass must have been dropped—but I never even noticed the major crack in the peg box that holds the strings on my bass. After a couple days of cold, dry weather, though, the crack began to get worse, though it only became noticeable *during* the concert. The peg box pulled forward, reducing the tension on my strings and making the pitch go flat! That's right: my bass was falling apart in my hands!

I played the first three pages of the piece without incident. After the first movement, though, I felt something funny. I checked my tuning and found the top string had gone down almost a quarter of a tone. I didn't understand why that was happening. I quickly adjusted the tuning peg for the next movement, and then noticed it was still losing pitch as I played. (For those who don't play a string instrument: you need to know that if the string is flat, the note you are looking for will be lower down on the instrument than you expect. Happy hunting!)

So now I was facing one of the biggest challenges of my lifetime. There were 2,500 people in the audience about to listen to this solo melody—which would sound terrible if played out of tune. And it was the difficult melody that I had practiced so hard and loud the night before. My bass was constantly going out of tune, and there was nothing I could do to fix it before I got to the magic passage. Yet I had to do *something*. I didn't want to stop the concert.

Then Allaudin's message came back to me, and I thought to myself: *Keep singing—sing louder than you play*! And there I was, attempting to find notes on a bass that were no longer where they are usually located!

Allaudin's solution was certainly demanding, but it was *possible*. Do you remember the *Mary Had a Little Lamb* story?

There were no frets on my bass, just the one pathetic, dying string. But that string was still like my vocal chord, and if I could just play that string like an extension of my vocal chord, I'd find the notes in relation to each other even though they would be located in some pretty strange places. *Forget the bass*, I told myself, *just play the string and the melody*! I started to sing (softly) while I played, but I realized that if that didn't work I'd have to start singing very loud to cover up my bass playing. Fortunately, my singing allowed my fingers to find their places on that one string, and I was able to get through the passage.

Whew! I must have lost ten pounds during that concert. But I gained a lesson that I will never forget. *Sing! Sing! Sing!*

Sing Louder, but also Play Softer

And here's another lesson which fits right in with the last one.

The great jazz bassist John Clayton often tells his students that when they are taking an improvised solo they should always play softer than those around them. Frankly, this didn't make much sense to me at first. Why would the soloist want to play softer than the other members of the ensemble? Well, after I'd given it some thought, I saw that he was right. If you are playing louder than your rhythm section or the harmony chords, how are you going to play in tune or in time with them? You have to be sensitive to the others so you can fit in with the musical texture of the group as a whole.

This is a delicate balance that we have to achieve. The inner voice needs to control the outer voice, and the outer voice has to find its balance within the larger ensemble and not drown out the other players!

Back to Resonance

Our bodies are like a sacred temple that can convert the air we breathe into pure vibration which is an affirmation of the spirit in music. Most people love feeling that they are part of a community, and joining together so that the group experience enhances and reaffirms our individual experiences. This is one of the reasons people of common faith want to get together to sing and worship.

Far more people participate in choral singing than in any other performing art, as a 2003 Music Educators National Conference study of Choruses in America revealed. Based on a random national poll of 1,000 adults and children, the report found that in 18% percent of households, one or more adults had performed publicly in a chorus within the previous year—which translates to 28.5 million adults and children nationally in the United States. The report established that there are approximately 250,000 choirs and choruses in the United States: 12,000 professional and community choruses, at least 38,000 school choruses, and 200,000 church choirs. Indeed, there are probably more choruses than any other kind of performing arts organization in this country.

Why do you think so many people participate in singing in choirs? Jerry Warren, Executive Director of the American Choral Directors Association, believes that singing creates a strong sense of relationship with feelings that are often explicit in the words and integrated with melody, harmony and rhythm. Warren says the key element is the emotion that drives those feelings. And once again, we see the resonance between our feelings and our physical participation.

Almost eighty percent of the people actively singing in America are participating in church choirs, and it's pretty clear to me that the concept of resonance applies to more than just the physical experience of singing—that it also includes both social and spiritual resonance. Furthermore, our music connections can be accompanied by non-musical inspirations such as faith and devotion.

While singing during a church service, the inspiration and desire to be connected to a higher power can dominate the musical experience. People can be and are inspired, regardless of whether they are singing in tune. Local congregations often allow those who have no special training as musicians to participate. They may not be able to read music, but they can pick up on nonverbal cues from nearby singers or the choir director and can attune their singing to that of their more highly skilled colleagues. Most importantly, they can legitimately contribute by feeling the music and expressing their emotions in song.

People who sing together typically work very hard to sing perfectly in tune with one another. It's not just about singing a song or playing a concert; it's about achieving a moment of connection.

The Breath Resonates Within

I like to think of it this way: the sails of a boat capture the ocean wind and turn it into motion, and windmills take the wind's power and transform it into available energy. When this same air enters our bodies and is recycled through our imagination, the air we inhale can resonate our vocal cords and vibrate our bodies so that it becomes imbued with new meaning as it is exhaled.

There is a wonderful energy that's possible when our vibrating vocal cords or external instruments are perfectly in tune with our inner voice. This is the essence of resonance. And breath is the heart of inspiration.

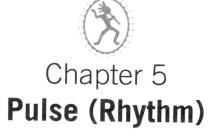

Chapter 5
Pulse (Rhythm)

Rhythm is the essence of life, from the heartbeat to the cycle of seasons to the symphony of sounds in nature. Its power goes beyond social and cultural boundaries to bind all living things on earth. The drum, in its universal expression, speaks to the soul of all people. It has been here for hundreds of years and is found in almost every culture... The language of rhythm is universal. The goal is empowerment, enlightenment and inspiration for people in all walks of life.

—Beverly Botsford

Our heartbeat is our life. After a heart attack, a car crash or in battle, any time we suspect that someone is dead, we listen for their heartbeat, try to take their pulse. And when that precious pulse is there, no matter how faint, when we can hear that heart beating, we know the person is still alive. The heartbeat is literally that crucial.

It shouldn't surprise us, then, that music begins from the heartbeat just as much as it does from the breath.

Grateful Dead drummer Mickey Hart puts it this way in his book *Planet Drum* (Harper Collins):

Music starts from this inner pulse—the heartbeat, the blood running, an awareness of how I feel. When you are playing inside of the pulse, you can anticipate or relax, and you produce different emotions. When you speed up, you are anticipating. When you slow down, you are relaxed and secure, producing a different kind of groove, not just a steady metronomic beat. Billy Kreutzmann calls it massaging the beat.

This chapter focuses on the essence of pulse, groove and rhythm as they relate to musical artistry.

Connecting with the pulse of music can be as simple as being consciously aware of it. When we focus on any recurring pulse it draws our attention and engages our body in the very spirit of the music. And as we become conscious of the pulse in music, in our bodies and in the colleagues we are playing or singing with, we begin to benefit from the artistic power of the musical groove. There is a special moment when the pulse comes alive in our bodies and in our music.

Rhythm Is Everywhere

Anything we can do that heightens our awareness and helps us internalize the pulses of the outside world will make us better musicians. Masanko Bando, a native of Malawi, Africa, an international peace-builder, educator, singer, dancer and drummer, told me:

Growing up as a child, the drum is the basic instrument. We as a people have always been surrounded and tapped into the "heartbeat." We spend nine months under our mother's heartbeat and then we come out in the world, everything around us has a pulse which we understand like a duck takes to water. The notion that Africans are born with rhythm is because we are born on our mothers' back. There is a difference from being raised in a stroller, rather being raised on your mother's back. Fetching water, chopping firewood, cooking, pounding corn, millet, doing the wash, working in the fields, all have their own rhythm. This writes into your psychology.

We can begin this process by noting how much vibration and rhythm surrounds us at almost every moment of the day. As I look outside my patio door I can see the trees swaying in the wind. If I watch the leaves, I can sense a steady sway of movement: it is slow, but contains a pulse. Listen to clocks, cars and construction machinery. Can you hear a recurring rhythmic sound in each case?

Dave Brubeck described one of his first inspirations for making music in *The Mastery of Music* (chapter 10: Creativity): the sound of a water pump, way out on the range when he was a kid, and then car windshield wipers, driving over a bridge, the rhythm of his horse's feet—even the rhythm of the name of a good friend like Marian McPartland—on which he based a song.

We have plenty of opportunities every day to notice our own personal rhythms. Talk a walk and listen to your feet hitting the ground: *left, right, left, right*. That's a simple recurring beat. You will find that most of the time there are at least two parts to any rhythm: there's the big beat we might call *one*, and then there can be subdivisions of that beat. In music, depending on the style, there could be multiple subdivisions of a rhythmic pattern, but it's best to start by finding the major pulse. There is something special about the power of that *one* in all the rhythms you'll find in music and in the world.

When you listen to music you may find it helpful to just nod your head in time with that big pulse, and there is a good possibility you will find the most common pulse is around sixty to ninety beats per minute—fairly close to the human heartbeat.

Here are some things you can do to start paying attention to pulse:

Activity: Finding the Pulse

1. Take a walk.
    a. Notice the rhythm you're creating as you move your feet.
    b. Begin by speaking each step aloud: "Left, right, left, right."
    c. Notice your left foot, and say "Left, left, left" as it hits the ground.
    d. Now just nod your head in time with your left foot hitting the ground.
2. Now notice every third step and the patterns that your awareness shows you:
    a. **Left,** right, left
       Right, left, right
       Left, right, left
    b. Try being aware of every fourth, fifth, or sixth step.
        i. Notice the different patterns that the first step creates each time:
           One, two, three, four
           Two, two, three four
           Three, two, three, four
           Four, two, three, four…and so on.
3. Every time you come back to *One* from two, three or more steps, you will find you are becoming aware of multiple rhythms—rhythms that in music we call 2/4, 3/4, and 4/4 time signatures.

4. Listen to AM radio and pay attention to the speed at which a talk radio host speaks.
   a. Listen to an AM radio commercial; and check out the tempo!
   b. Can you hear both the words themselves and the larger divisions of the tempo?
5. Now listen to FM radio. Notice that the speed of speech is much slower.
   a. Does it make you feel any different as you listen?
6. Say your name over and over while you walk in tempo.
   a. Notice the rhythm and the pulse.
   b. The start of each repetition of your name gives you the basic pulse, while the syllables of your name create rhythm within that pulse.
7. Listen to some music.
   a. Tap your foot to the pulse or nod your head to and fro.
   b. Now feel the basic pulse in the head, shoulders and feet.
   c. Use your hand to tap out the faster rhythms.

The Power of Pulse, Groove and Rhythm

As we become more aware of the pulse, tempo and rhythm in the sounds we hear throughout the day we may want to join in with the rhythm. Sadly, there's a voice in the mind that tells us not to. And that's a real problem, not just because we're shutting down a natural expression of human energy and vitality, but because it may actually make us lethargic. When you allow your body to groove to the rhythm, you are likely to feel more alive!

The word *rhythm* comes from the Greek word *rhythmos,* meaning measured motion. It's also akin to the Greek *rhein,* meaning flow.

It's the flow I feel that's the Groove. When a stream flows it is one with itself, flowing around bends, going faster, slower—it's always one stream. When we play music and the Groove happens, we are one—like the stream.

To illustrate how an individual becomes one with the Universe, Eastern philosophy often uses the analogy of a drop of water and the ocean. The drop has individual and separate characteristics, but when it merges with the ocean it becomes the ocean. When we enter the Groove it is much the same.

When we groove, we feel connected. This is why we enjoy going to sports events, concerts and other public gatherings. Expressing appreciation by clapping our hands is a rhythmic experience that connects us to our feelings, with those we admire and with those around us. Imagine yourself at a football game chanting "DE-fence, DE-fence, DE-fence." You're repeating the word over and over with intensity and emotion, with rhythm. That repeated pulse just has a way of getting into our emotions...

Robert Wallace is a wonderful drummer and teacher whose Total Rhythm classes include fitness along with all manner and styles of drumming. Robert has worked with my Bass Camp students on movement and rhythm, and says:

The Power of Rhythm is the Power of Repetition. When we lock into a beat, our mind *slows down* (and, ultimately, turns off) and we reconnect with our physical rhythm: heartbeat, breath, and muscle movement. We stop looking outside of ourselves for stimulation and approval; we begin to listen to the still, calm voice from inside. Some call this intuition, guidance, love, or even God. I call it my soul, my life force, or my "axe" ("ah-shay") as they say in Brazil.

This energy is inside every one of us, and it is constantly attempting to share its wisdom and guidance. Unfortunately, most of the time we are too busy, too much into "More, Faster, Now"—so we seldom stop to listen. And that's too bad, because this message from our spirit is exactly what we *need* and *want* to hear, in order to live our lives in complete accord with our dreams and desires.

You'll start hearing it and feeling it yourself when you tap into the Power of Rhythm.

Connecting with Others through Rhythm

In chapter 4 on Breath we explored our need to spend time in community and *resonate* with others through chanting and singing. We can meet this same need through drumming—and indeed, often the two are linked together, and that is wonderful. Either way, it often feels good to be part of something bigger than ourselves—to be linked in community.

Robert Wallace writes:

People have gathered for thousands of years, in virtually every culture on the planet, to *drum together*. Human beings don't do *anything* for a long time unless it has a benefit, and rhythm provides a tremendous benefit. Group drumming creates a supported place where we not only connect with our own spirit we *then share this experience with others*. We are no longer alone or isolated. Rather, we collectively feed our souls, our higher selves, through the beat. And what a meal! Locking in complimentary rhythms, and holding those beats tight like a muscle is incredibly powerful, even thrilling. Many skills are needed to make this happen:

We must be willing to go to a deeper place first individually and then collectively,

We must listen to each other,

We must communicate with each other in the context of a unifying beat.

Mindful Drumming and Kokomon Clottey

Drumming circles, which may have their roots in African or other indigenous cultures, are becoming increasingly popular in American culture. In today's high-paced, technologically sophisticated and increasingly materialistic life, the drumming experience provides an escape into a world of peace, community and brotherhood. Our decision-makers and politicians often look toward higher education in science and technology for an answer to social unrest and violence, but the best examples of peace, brotherhood, community and just simple listening to one another are to be found in the arts. The quickest way to settle into the moment, escape the worries and pride and respond with mind, body and spirit is just to find the beat and join in!

In West Oakland, Kokomon Clottey's Attitudinal Healing Center gives troubled youth opportunities for self expression and creativity by getting them involved in drumming circles, arts and crafts, poetry and fashion design. In one of Kokomon's Mindful Drumming circles, the focus is on twenty or more adults in a circle following a single rhythmic course as they play the African drum called the djembe.

I have witnessed the power of this continuing rhythm on the state of my mind. We repeated each rhythmic pattern given to us by the leader for three to five minutes before shifting to another pattern. And instead of fretting about politics, gas prices or the grocery list, the mind just sinks into the feeling of community and rests in the beat. At the end of a one-hour, non-stop drumming class repeating simple rhythmic patterns together, each of us had an opportunity to share our feelings and experiences, and a diverse community of educators, professionals, parents and blue- and white-collar workers from the greater Oakland community spoke as if they had awakened from a dream. Each of us in turn shared our gratitude for this hour in which we could leave our troubles, agendas, work and family concerns behind and escape into the bliss enabled by sound and rhythm within the circle.

I call this our "music church" because the rhythm of the drums brings us the inspiration and opportunity to connect one another in an unselfish and generous way as a community. And another thing—I found as a musician that I really appreciated hearing my own sound disappear into the sound of the large group. I could no longer hear my own individual sound, and I had no wish to. Instead, I found myself moving and grooving as part of the great, rich, full sound that was making the entire room vibrate. I just surrendered to the movement, to the beat, to the feeling in the circle—and it felt healing, inspiring and life-giving. It felt as though my sound had melted into the group sound and somehow the group sound had become my sound, too.

As the great African drummer Babatunde Olatunji said in his video, *African Drumming* (Warner Brothers),

The spirit of the drum is something that you feel but you cannot put your hands on. It does something to you from the inside out. It hits people in so many different ways. But the feeling is one that is satisfying and joyful. It is a feeling that makes you say to yourself, "I'm glad to be alive today! I'm glad to be part of this world!"

And the beauty of this experience is that it is so simple that it is available to everyone. You don't have to have a great drumming technique or even own a djembe to participate.

Beverly Botsford and Drumming as a Spiritual Experience

Beverly Botsford, cross-cultural percussionist and band colleague of soul singer Nnenna Freelon, reminded me how we calm a crying baby: the first and most obvious way is to cradle it to your body and either rock it back and forth or pat it gently on the back with a steady, loving pulse. And what works for the infant, perhaps not surprisingly, can also touch life's greatest heights: the power of the groove can be a spiritual and transformational experience.

When I interviewed her, Botsford asked me:

Why is there so much power inside a groove?

Rhythm is transformation—think of the heartbeat, and of the great cycles of earth and sky. When you look for a common factor in spiritual practices all over the world, you'll find the groove. The power of the groove in rhythm is the major spiritual practice in all cultures. Spirit possession happens in so many cultures through the groove. It makes transformation happen on a lot of levels, and there may even be a chemical side to it—and if you go to the AME

116

Zion church, you won't have the Holy Ghost come without that inspirational groove!

What all this boils down to is that I encourage you join a drumming circle in your community. Do a web search for "drumming circles in <your town>." And if you join a circle, perhaps the easiest preparation would be to allow your hands to make an equal sound from left to right: that's a great start.

Here is a simple way to build this equal connection with your two hands which I have borrowed with permission from the Music for People manual *Return to Child* by Jim Oshinsky—a rich source of exercises for building rhythm skills.

Activity: Even-handed Drumming

1. Use a hand drum (such as a conga, djembe, etc.) if possible. Otherwise, use body percussion by drumming on your knees.
2. Begin at a slow and comfortable speed.
3. Start a pulse by alternating your right and left hands on the drum.
4. Lift your hands and let them fall naturally, one after the other.
5. Listen deeply to the sound each hand makes, and strive to have your dominant and non-dominant hands make identical sounds.
6. Experiment with how loosely you hold your wrists and fingers, and whether your hands are flat to the drumhead or slightly tilted.
7. Cupping your hands will change the timbre of the sound.

There are many excellent instructional videos that can help you with hand drumming techniques. Some of them feature the best percussionists in recent history, both living and deceased. For African drumming, I recommend the late Baba Olatunji's video. For frame drumming, see the videos of Glen Velez. For Brazilian percussion, check out Robert Wallace's DVD on Pandeiro and Caxixi. Curt Moore's DVD is on Afro-Cuban drumming. All these DVDs are listed in the resources section at the back of the book.

A Musician's Best Friend: the Metronome!

While this chapter is dedicated to creating a relationship between the heart, body and soul through the pulse of the music, you can help this bond along by becoming a friend of that inexpensive mechanical device: the metronome! You can probably find one for an investment of less than twenty-five dollars, and with its help you can create a steady pulse, adjusting accents on every two, three, four or more beats.

Practicing in rhythm while gradually increasing tempo so that you avoid making mistakes allows your muscles to build physical memory, and that's good for your musical health! Becoming familiar with the tick of the metronome when there's no music playing may help you awaken your internal sense of groove when the metronome is silent. The ultimate goal is to be able to hear *or imagine* the metronome and feel its pulse so body and music can respond.

Pulse is like a river's current, which can support a boatful of people paddling together. We all have to put our oars in the water in a common rhythm to keep the boat moving, but we must also respect the speed of the current or we'll feel resistance and drag. Each one of us is only a small part of the larger musical whole.

Subdivisions: Sharing the Groove

What is so important is that when two or more people play together, they have to become in touch with the whole while playing their individual parts, and rhythm is what brings and keeps us together. Watch a large orchestra in performance: the conductor is like the brain and nervous system of a solo performer, and the orchestral musicians are the body. Conductors usually set the tempo, the speed of the music, and are also expected to offer direction in terms of musical style, phrasing and balance.

Watch any successful maestro and you will see them doing much more than just beating time with the right (baton) hand. You will see what I've been calling rhythmic subdivisions in other parts of the body. Watch the conductor's legs, shoulders, hips and head. Watch rock musicians, great chamber players, pop singers or jazz musicians and you will notice them moving various parts of their bodies to different subdivisions in the music—moving actively with the groove.

Here's the point: If you are going to be a part of the music, you have to be like a maestro and connect with the *entire* piece, all in one person! You do that by learning to divide yourself up and let different parts of your body (and breath) express *each* of these roles simultaneously. This may sound like a tall order—I know it might be simpler if you just had to learn your notes and play your part with the right dynamics and expression. But that won't bring the music to life.

I believe you have to become a master drummer, scholarly maestro, juggler, dancer, singer, actor and virtuoso all in one! And the amazing thing is that you can do it—I've seen it done, at every level from middle school and younger to professional musician and better. You need to bring complex rhythms and grooves with their multiple parts into your body regardless of the fact that you may actually only be *playing* one part of the rhythm in the eighth notes of the melody.

Do you recall Clark Terry's comment in *The Mastery of Music*? He said, "always keep your rhythm section in your hip pocket"— and it applies to the entire rhythm section! In *Bringing Music to Life*, whether performing as a soloist or in a duo, trio or large ensemble, each individual musician has to embody *all* the working elements of the rhythm and pulse.

When you are playing in an orchestra, band or choir, you are always serving a double function: playing your part in the harmony, melody or counterpoint, but also being part of the rhythmic groove.

Percussionist and educator Curt Moore, the author of the DVD *Afro-Cuban Drum Set: Grooves You Can Use*, helped me explore these rhythmic concepts with three high school orchestras in the San Francisco Bay area. In the course of the program Curt was able to extract the rhythm from the harmonies and melodies in the music of Schubert, Tchaikovsky, Bernstein and Copland. His students reduced their notes to rhythmic clapping, tapping bows on tailpieces or vocalizing syllables such as *da* and *ta* until all heard their own parts as a whole rhythm section with essential subdivisions hidden in the melodies, countermelodies and harmonies.

By reducing notes to pure rhythmic strokes and then bringing back melodic or harmonic qualities, these students were able to tighten their ensemble playing and make music together at a new level of perfection.

Following a Changing Pulse in Your Breath and Upper Body

While we can think of rhythm as a container that supports harmony and melody, it doesn't always have to remain rigid or inflexible. Different styles of music demand different approaches to pulse. Classical music can have gradual *accelerando* or *ritard* and other spontaneous movements. Jazz music as well as rock, hip-hop or rap is often associated with a more fixed pulse/groove. Contemporary classical and world music from different cultures all have their own relationship to pulse, but the groove will still have an internal tightness: it just doesn't have to always be steady.

Multicultural percussion specialist Ian Dogole, who plays with many world music performers in the San Francisco Bay Area, described playing Indian music with distinguished colleagues:

When I had the good fortune to play with Hamza El Din (the great Indian oud virtuoso, the oud being the Arab precursor of the lute) with Allaudin Mathieu on piano and Jean Jeanrenaud on cello, the pulse was always changing and in constant flux. We are playing Nubian music, from southern Egypt and the northern Sudan region of the Nile. As a jazz musician you want to be exactly on time—but here the time was moving from bar to bar, and I had to play in synch with Hamza El Din. It was like weeds bending in the wind—but the pulse was in flux!

Well, I learned that isn't a bad thing, because to be musical you have to be flexible! It was all about listening to where he is going faster or slower, and learning to like it. And it got to a point where I felt great playing this exquisite, tranquil music with a flexible pulse.

Ian also talked about how important it is to be free and relaxed in order to sustain any kind of groove.

> When the group is breathing together, that's when the greatest music is taking place. It has this effortless quality. It is so important to eliminate as much tension out of your body as possible. If I am breathing and loose, then I have the ability to *relax* into the time. Relaxation allows me to play for long periods of time without being tired—and still having the pulse be solid. And it is also important to quiet my mind and eliminate inner chatter that takes me out of my zone!

I have often been given the advice *Put the pulse in your feet, Tap your foot!* and *Keep the rhythm!* But when I talk about this with my son Adam, a professional percussionist with one of the premiere military concert bands in Washington DC, he reminds me that the feet are a long way from the center of the body where we internalize the pulse. Watch musicians tapping their feet and you may notice their rhythm isn't very accurate! Adam suggests that the pulse can be felt best when it comes from the area around the chest and heart.

Sometimes, too, when musicians are playing on a large stage and separated by considerable distances, they have to trust visual cues to read where the pulse is.

Adam says:

> You don't want to rely on foot tapping. I like to see the heads bobbing, the flow of arms and upper body as a visual reference. It is a more effective way of getting an accurate pulse—by looking and seeing what is going on, rather than relying on what you hear.

When I feel a groove I feel it in my heart, and my chest, which is where I bounce. When you are using your arms and fingers on an instrument or drum, they are directly connected to your chest. That connection to the pulse comes from the center of your body. If you are dancing and grooving it is pivoting around your body core, and that's the easiest place to feel the groove.

Bob Becker, world famous multi-percussionist with the percussion ensemble Nexus, has spent many years studying Indian music in general and the tabla in particular. There is a tradition of teaching the tabla through the vocalization of set syllables that represent every sound of the drum.

Becker explains:

This vocal tradition of articulating the sounds that are played on the tabla is a very interesting and powerful experience, both for learning and more importantly for memorizing. Over the course of fifteen years of intense study of tabla, I probably memorized several hundred pieces, something I had never done before. This was a powerful connection between the mnemonic vocalization (using vocal syllables to approximate the different sounds of the tabla) and the body. When you learn to speak a rhythmic pattern, you can transfer it to your hands. Now I have learned the process by studying tabla, I've experienced it with African drumming as well as the snare drum. It's the best possible interface between the instruments and myself.

These are the same principles discussed in chapter 4 on breath that keep the music as close as possible to the source of the center of our body. *If you can sing it, you can play it.* The internalization of music into the breath and voice can facilitate a more direct connection to our extremities—and with those instruments on the ends of our hands and feet!

Remember that *you* are the one who plays the music, and it must first come through your body. When we hold an instrument in our hands (or feet), it is far from the center of our body core. Intensifying the inner voice by internal vocalization of the rhythm helps intensify and speed the transmission of this sound through our bodies. And when it reaches our hands, feet and fingers and is finally transferred to our drums, pianos, string and wind instruments, the music is still alive!

Sharing the Groove

In a *Mindful Drumming* session with Kokomon Clottey, everyone in a large group primarily embraces one rhythmic pattern, playing exactly the same rhythm so that the whole group sounds like a single person playing on one enormous drum. It may be surprising to think of powerful drumming that way, but there is in fact great meditative power in this experience: the mind just naturally relaxes as we enter into unison with the larger group.

Much of our music requires us to share the pulse with other drummers or instrumentalists. One half of the group may be playing on beats 1 and 2 while the other half plays on beats 3 and 4—so you're always doing one or the other, but not both—but the sound in the room is four steady quarter notes.

Your body should internalize the sound and groove of the two beats that you are *not* playing along with the two that you are, but you play only the two beats of your part. This is what goes on with most ensembles when rhythm parts are broken up and shared among players. When you share part of a groove or rhythm with other players you learn to balance your part with the group so that it seems as though the music is all coming from the same place and played by just one person.

When this works well, all the contributing players are listening to each other and playing as one.

Activity: Sharing the Rhythm with Your Body

In this exercise we follow four rhythmic sounds, but not at the same time. The overall pattern is based on making four different sounds on four beats.

1. Stomp both your feet (or heels) on the ground on beat 1.
2. Slap your knees with your hands on beat 2.
3. Clap your hands together on beat 3.
4. Snap your fingers on beat 4.
5. Repeat this pattern several times.

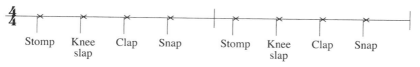

Example 5.1.

Reflection

1. While each sound is different and comes from a different part of your body, did you notice the four sounds coming together to form a greater rhythmic pattern across the four consecutive beats?

2. Focus equally on these four consecutive sounds rather than on the production of any single one of them.

3. Now make the hand clap louder than the other sounds and notice how this impacts your sense of the overall pattern as a whole.

4. Make the knee slap louder and notice this sound—but don't hurt yourself!

5. Go back and see if you can make all the sounds equal in volume.

Another variation of this activity involves a group of participants—this can be a band, orchestra, chorus or just a group of more than four people. In this exercise:

1. Divide your group in four parts.

2. The goal is to have everyone in the group clap with an equal volume and in equal rhythm.

3. While each person claps on a different beat, all need to be in touch with the sound of the entire group so that both the volume and the rhythm remain equal.

4. Adjust the volume or dynamics of your clap so that the combined sound of the whole group is the same.

Activity: Sharing the Rhythm with Others in an Ensemble

1. Group 1 claps on beats 1 and 2.

2. Group 2 claps on beats 2 and 3.

3. Group 3 claps on beats 3 and 4.

4. Group 4 claps on beats 4 and 1.

5. Repeat this pattern until your sound disappears into the group and you hear an even clapping among all four groups.

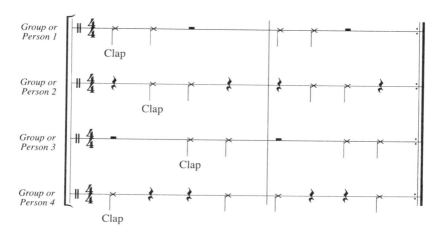

Example 5.2.

A second variation of this is to clap *twice* on the eighth note pulse (twice as quickly) but on only one beat.

1. Group 1 claps twice on beat 1 (two eighth notes).
2. Group 2 claps twice on beat 2 (two eighth notes).
3. Group 3 claps twice on beat 3 (two eighth notes).
4. Group 4 claps twice on beat 4 (two eighth notes).

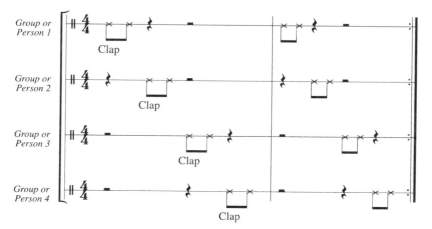

Example 5.3.

In both of these activities (and you can create many other variations on these basic patterns), one steady-pulse pattern is created and divided up between more than one person. When you are playing or singing in any ensemble, it is important for you to know and notice when your rhythmic groove is shared with others and to make sure you are able to tap into the combined sound and balance of everyone sharing that groove.

Look at this rap pattern from Allaudin Mathieu's *Stomp!* and notice how each instrument shares a part of the groove!

Example 5.4. *Heart, Soul & Stomp,* movement 3: "Stomp," W. A. Mathieu

If you are participating in an ensemble of more than four people, such as a string, wind, brass or vocal ensemble, notice whether your part is based on a subdivision of the overall rhythm. While you might be playing a melody or some harmony, your part might *also* be based on rhythms that make up part of the larger groove.

Your goal is to increase your awareness of your role as part of the larger rhythmic unit. When you notice that you are part of the larger whole you can play with new insight, balance and musicality, and the musical end result will be steady and balanced!

You may notice that something special happens when you are sharing three or more parts of a combined groove with other musicians—as is the case in example 5.4. Two parts together work well, but when the third and fourth parts enter, something magical happens because of the blending of so many people playing so many different interlocking patterns.

Beverly Botsford talks about this electric energy:

The individuality of each of the parts working in its own special way makes it rock so heavy. When all the parts combine and become one beautifully designed groove, rich with diversity, it all transforms into its own amazing entity. It is so deep and special a thing to be a part of a whole that you could never create by yourself. That's when transformation happens!

We have been progressively building our understanding and participation of the pulse to include:

1. A unison pulse (mindful drumming).
2. A simple, steady pulse created within yourself (body percussion).
3. A simple, steady pulse shared by two or more people.
4. A more complex pulse shared by four or more people.

The final step includes internalizing a complex rhythm through your body *while* you are actually playing a harmonic or melodic part. In effect, we are all simultaneously playing *all* the music— harmony, melody and rhythm! Does that sound outrageous? You can often *see* this when great musicians perform. This is what they are doing—it's what makes their music come to life.

Watch jazz singers. Watch Latin players groove with their bodies, singing along when they are *not* actually playing—but listening to others soloing at the same time! Watch drummers when they are playing their parts, but also notice them catching the eyes of other musicians.

If the groove is not alive in your body, it will not be alive in your music.

Now that we are more aware of rhythms and subdivisions we need to find a way to internalize our rhythmic sense and let it move in our bodies while we are playing just our own part of the music— perhaps a melody or a part of the rhythm. This means being aware of every other sound that is happening while you play your part.

Here is a simple example of how you can do this: chose one or more of the songs in examples 5.4–5.6 and allow yourself to subdivide the rhythm in your body while singing the melody. Have fun!

Activity: Subdivided Rhythm in the Body and Melody in the Voice

You may find it easier to get the rhythm going for a while before you start singing.

Exercise A: Rock Music

Pulse:	Quarter note. Tap your foot or chest, or bob your head.
Steady eighth notes:	Gently slap your leg.
Theme in quarter and eighth notes:	Sing this part.

Example 5.5. Rock Music

Exercise B: Folk Music. *Turkey in the Straw*

Pulse:	Quarter note: Tap your foot or chest, or bob your head.
Eighth note off-beats on each beat:	Gently slap your leg.
Melody sixteenth notes:	Sing the sixteenth notes to the syllables *da-ga-da-ga*.

Example 5.6. Folk Music. *Turkey in the Straw*

Exercise C: Jazz Music. *Blue Moon*

Pulse: Quarter note: Tap your foot or chest, or bob your head.

Subdivision,
eighth note pattern: Swing beat like triplet: long, short, long-short-long on beats 2 and 4, like a cymbal pattern on a drum set.

Melody: Sing the melody: *Blue Moon*

Blue Moon,
You saw me standing alone
Without a dream in my heart,
Without a love of my own…

Example 5.7. Jazz Music. *Blue Moon*

Reflection

1. What did you notice when you had all of the pulse going in your body and you began to sing?
2. When you started to sing were you confused by the rhythms in your body? If so, stay with the rhythms longer before starting to sing.
3. What did it feel like to engage in the song without thinking of the rhythm in your body?
4. How did if feel to be completely absorbed in your chosen tune?

Holding the Groove Is Everyone's Responsibility

Perhaps you are improvising a solo in a funk or jazz style. Maybe you are playing a melody over an exciting rhythmic groove in Shostakovich's *Fifth Symphony. Keeping the rhythm section in your hip pocket* also means that if the rhythm players stop and you are still playing, you have a responsibility to keep that groove going.

Jeff Hamilton is one of the world's greatest jazz drummers, co-leader of the Clayton-Hamilton Jazz Orchestra and a favorite drummer with Ray Brown, Oscar Petersen, and many other world famous jazz icons! Jeff feels that everyone in any band has an *equal* responsibility to hold the groove. He says:

> I don't like it when one person dictates the tempo. Each player has to participate in the groove equally. Can you play it alone? Can you be responsible for the tempo? Can you hold it yourself? When that happens, you don't have players laying over you, leading you around. This is a community effort, and we are all supposed to be in this together.

Bringing the Groove to Life!

We have explored elements of pulse and rhythm as they exist in nature, our bodies and lives. This pulse can be experienced and expressed in groups such as drum circles and can impact our state of consciousness.

We have seen how rhythmic groove can be performed by one person or shared by more players. Most importantly, we must remember that *everyone* must participate in the creation of rhythm even if they are playing a melody that soars above the groove. Jeff Hamilton told me that when he played with Ray Brown, Ray's bass lines were melodies. Jeff loved to sing those bass lines while he was playing time on his drum set.

So rhythm players key into the groove and sing along with the melody, too! And melody players have to be able to hold the groove all by themselves and let the groove live in their bodies as well. *Everyone* needs to be in touch with the totality of the music regardless of the particular part they are playing.

But while we can follow all these instructions, multitrack, sing, play, tap our feet, beat our chest and bob our heads, this doesn't guarantee the presence of artistic energy or life in our music. The final element that has to be present is all about sincerity, integrity and perhaps most of all, intensity! And that, too, is a matter of pulse.

When you hear great music and are inspired by the groove, the life in that groove is vivid in its clarity and strength. If you watch great jazz musicians, classical artists or performers of any style of music you can sometimes see sweat coming from their brows or hear groaning or breathing as they perform. These things happen because they are at a level of acute intensity which is integral and fundamental to the vividness and clarity of their art.

Jeff Hamilton says a drummer has to *show intensity* in the beat that matches the inner voice. Jeff also mentions that a drummer should be able to sing the cymbal pattern—the bassist should be able to sing the bass line—out loud, before playing it. There has to be energy that draws in the listener.

A Vocal Technique for Instrumentalists

There is another vocal technique for instrumentalists—this is *not* recommended for singers!—which they can use to intensify their musical roles. It's called the *Grrrr*. When you begin to growl or groan as you play, your body gets the sense that you mean business.

This is a technique that's used a lot in jazz circles. When students are asked to groan or act like they are mad, the result is immediate, increased intensity. Louie Belson calls groaning or growling the *fifth independent limb* for drummers. Since they are already playing with four limbs—two hands and two feet—a good growl or groan pushes them into a kind of fifth gear of intensity. Jeff Hamilton puts it this way:

> When I'm standing six feet from a musician and can hear them singing or groaning as they play, I feel good. Those people are really my favorite players. They aren't just applying their talent to the music; they are making it an entire body experience. Without this intensity, it's like a stone skipping across water but never getting beneath the surface into the real depths.

135

I remember playing my first ballad with Ray Brown and Oscar Petersen in July of 1990 at the Hollywood Bowl. It was the second tune of the night. I was sweating through my tuxedo, and all of us in the bandstand were growling Grrrrrrhhh!!!! That's how intense the beat was on this ballad. If you know your intensity and your groove, it will dig its heels into where it needs to be, without you trying to force it.

Intensity, discipline, integrity, commitment and concentration are inseparable partners in bringing a groove to life. So we strive to find a comfortable place that will allow mind, voice and body to embrace all the elements of pulse and bring them into a conscious union where our part is one with the whole.

That is where the life of the pulse is to be found!

Bob Becker feels one of the key ingredients in bringing a pulse to life is in each individual's *commitment to every sound* that is made:

Nothing is thrown away and nothing at all is without intent. And that takes a lot of experience and a whole lot of specific practice. This is not part of our usual training. Every musician has to commit individually to this way of playing. If you do that and get used to doing that, then you can play with enormous authority. That's what's most gratifying for any performer or group of performers.

It's also what's most powerful, moving, and exciting for the audience.

Being in the Flow Is Like Being Played by the Music

The pulse, the groove, the rhythm really does have a mystical power to transform music, to connect our bodies and souls to its flow and carry us to a state of bliss. The pulse demands that we surrender to its repetitive power. It has its own tempo and its own life. And while we can certainly influence it, we should not be overly controlling. It is best when we participate in it but honor and respect its strength and groove. *Letting it happen* allows the life in the music to reach us. *Making it happen* disturbs the flow and diminishes its strength.

It is truly a magical moment when music takes on a life of its own. We are lost in the music, and for those precious moments we are free of the burden of individual identity. We are listening with our ears wide open—and the total product is bigger and more profound than any one individual part. Ian Dogole describes the state like this:

> For me, I'm going into a state of ecstasy. I'm in this blissful state where I don't have to do much any more. The pulse has a life of its own. I could leave my body and my hands would keep right on playing. The group is breathing together; the soloists are playing to their highest level. The music is playing me, and boy do I love that! There is such joy in this process.

It's all in the pulse.

Chapter 6
Movement (Body)

The truest expression of a people is in its dance and in its music. Bodies never lie.

—Agnes de Mille

Can you imagine Mick Jagger sitting perfectly still with no expression whatsoever on his face? I suppose you can, but it's not easy—Mick's whole genius in his gift of movement, and we hardly ever see him sitting still, let alone looking bored or vacant! He's a musician, and he's a mover! When he rocks, he *rocks!* And you know, when the virtuoso violinist Joshua Bell plays a soaring melody, his body, too, seems to soar as he carries his audience with him somewhere else, somewhere beyond. Joshua Bell is a musician and a mover, too…

The late maestro Leonard Bernstein conducted his orchestras with fire, passion and grace: he was a musician and a mover. His twenty-first century counterpart, the Venezuelan conductor Gustavo Dudamel is the same: he communicates with his players through vivid body gestures. And you know something about all these folks? They're not just musicians who happen to be movers; the way they move is part and parcel of their musicianship.

Have you seen Pancho Sanchez, Tito Puente, Shelia E or Pete Escovido play the drums? Can you sit still while they play, sing and dance?

Opera Diva Frederica von Stade delivers her golden voice through her heart, body and soul, causing Timothy Pfaff of the *Los Angeles Times* to write, "Watching her move, watching her act, hearing her sing is among the greatest experiences I have had." And when pianist Jon Kimura Parker played the Tchaikovsky *Piano Concerto* recently, the *South China Morning Post* in Hong Kong said he "used the piano stool as a biking seat, racing forward and, at times, standing up to transform the piano into his 'handle bars' as he headed into the sunset."

These are all examples of great artists who are master communicators because they engage the body while expressing their craft. I'm convinced that movement is the final piece of the puzzle—that a real sense of freedom to move with music is something we frequently undervalue, and that it may be the single most powerful element in bringing music to life.

The body-to-body connection is so primal in the arts that it deserves further exploration to see how we can embrace and integrate it through conscious, independent study. For some people this is so natural that it doesn't need to be discussed—but traditional music education leaves a huge gap as to who's responsible for teaching and encouraging the integration of the body into self-expression, whether it's classical, folk, jazz, improvisation or even pop music that's being taught.

And this does not reflect the natural way of things.

Childhood play is unfiltered and spontaneous and we respond to it directly and naturally. When we see a baby jump for joy we feel happy for them; when we watch them cry or stumble, we feel their pain. Early preschool music education encourages children to sing while banging on drums, blocks and bells, and while marching, moving or grooving to the pulse. But as soon as puberty sets in, all that freedom, all that bodily enthusiasm vanishes under the pressures of self-consciousness, doubt, judgment, peer pressure—the list is long—accountability to parents and teachers and those all-important test scores. The playing stops, and everyone gets serious!

Sooner or later a successful adult musician will find a way to return to that first, youthful, joyful, body-integrated approach—and that's why our greatest contemporary artists seem to express themselves with such youthful, reckless abandon. But in the meantime, our educational system creates obstacles to that kind of enthusiasm—and it's time for a new pedagogy that will avoid these obstacles and actively embrace movement in music.

Letting the Music Flow through the Body

The body should respond immediately to the requests of the mind. The less the gap between the two, the more efficient the action will be.

—Vanda Scaravelli, yoga master

Tai chi speaks of a flow of inspiration coming to us from the greater universe around us, and this flow of inspiration comes to us from sky and air, wind and breath, from the earth beneath our feet and the consciousness of spirit—and in making music, this world of inspiration is to be channeled through a composer's notes or though our own direct improvisation. Once we are quiet within ourselves and open to hearing and communicating the musical message, it must enter into the soul, heart, mind and muscles, and *leave* the body as an expression of art.

If the body is tight and inflexible, the music will be trapped inside.

Unfortunately, there are fewer exercises dedicated to embodying the spirit of music through movement than there are for breath and pulse-work—but here are several movement practices that I have found both inspiring and helpful.

The purest disciplines teaching music through movement are those of Jacques-Dalcroze's Eurhythmics and Orff-Schulwerk, both taught in accredited courses at music schools or though the independent licensing programs offered by the Dalcroze and Orff societies. For unfortunate social and political reasons, these fabulous methodologies are most frequently taught to preschool students when instead they need to be offered as part of every public school music program for students of all ages.

It is time for our community music schools to provide Eurhythmic and Orff classes for adults—but in the meantime we must find our own movement disciplines, often through attending programs that are more generally directed toward movement and less musically specific, programs that may have been developed within such complementary disciplines as exercise, meditation, dance, socializing or even spirituality.

Eurhythmics

We begin our journey with a practice that is available to music teachers in an academic environment and most commonly taught to young children: Eurhythmics.

Many of the Dalcroze Eurhythmics techniques are about making connections to the body with the final goal of using those connections in making music. Exploring the methodology involved will help us integrate some of the many other non-musically oriented systems that can inspire us to develop these connections. Eurhythmics tells us:

> The human body is the source of all musical ideas, and human movement affects musical perception. Eurhythmics (means "good rhythm") allows us to gain physical awareness and experience of music so training must take place through all

the senses (including the kinesthetic/body movement), not just focused on the mind.

Nicole Brockmann of DePauw University is a past president of the Dalcroze Society of America and has been using Dalcroze principles in coaching her college-level viola students. Knowing the method is most often associated with teaching young children, she reminded me that Jacques-Dalcroze developed his method out of frustration with the lack of energy flow through the bodies of his college-level students at the Geneva Conservatory. Nicole lamented the fact that Eurhythmics practice is reduced as kids get older, in part because they are more self-conscious about the body and in part, too, because parents may worry about their children being in physical contact with other children.

Brockmann explains the founding principles of Eurhythmics:

Students need to recognize early on that music isn't the sound the instrument makes, it doesn't come from the instrument, it comes from them. We use the body itself to explore the more abstract concepts of musicianship. We first work on expression, character, feelings, qualities, speeds, and energies while away from the instrument. We only begin to hold our instruments after we have brought these feelings into the body—only then do we begin to ask ourselves, how do we translate this into sound?

And once you fix a student's technical problems to an awareness of musical energy through movement, the student will generally find that the problems fall in place.

I asked Nicole to give me an example of a Eurhythmic exercise for bringing music into the body.

Activity: Moving to the "Funeral March" in Beethoven's *Seventh Symphony*

1. Walk (step) to the rhythm of the "Funeral March":
    tum–tumti–tum–tum
    tum–tumti–tum–tum

2. Take a step on each beat:
    left…right-left…right…left
    right…left-right…left…right

3. Notice how your body responds to the longer and shorter note lengths.

4. What are some descriptive words that fit the mood or emotional feel of this music?

5. What kinds of body feeling and movements do those words suggest?

6. Stop walking the ostinato and use your upper body to express the flowing melody that is linked to the rhythm.

7. Do the same kinds of words and body feeling come to mind?

8. Can you pay attention to both the ostinato and rhythm at once?

9. Switch back and forth between them.
    a. Try singing the melody while walking the ostinato, or
    b. using your upper body to express the qualities of the melody while tapping the ostinato with your toe.

This exercise engages the bodily perception of two contrasting moods of physical expression, with one part of you dedicated to the rhythmic pulse and the other to the flowing melody—and that's a critical skill: we need to be able to capture the whole of a piece of music in all parts of our bodies while perhaps expressing just one component of the music with our instrument.

Activity: Paying Attention to the Body while Hearing Music

1. Play any piece of music on your radio, CD or MP3 player.
2. What do you feel, moment by moment?
3. Can you put a word to these feelings?
4. Where do you feel tightness? expansion?
5. What does this music make you want to do?
    a. Fling your arms wide and open to the heavens?
    b. Curl up in a ball?
    c. Feel creepy and grab your stomach?
    d. Just settle down?

Nicole Bockmann told me, "You have to be willing to really listen and pay attention to what's going on in your body—and most grownups just aren't ready to do that." If it's uncomfortable for us, is it necessary? Let's take another look at some of the great performers mentioned in the first few paragraphs of this chapter. Are they comfortable in their bodies? I think the answer is a resounding "Yes." Indeed, I'm suggesting that movement is part of the territory that goes with being a performing artist—and it needs to be part of the training and discipline that is both normal and universal for our craft.

Tai Chi and Martial Arts Are Essential Gifts to Music

Tai chi master Chungliang Al Huang was the one who showed me how to let my body be the vessel for my music. He taught me that the music comes from outside the body, passes through it, then emerges back out into the world: *our body is the vessel for our creativity.* Now when I conduct a one- or two-day Inner Game of Music workshop, I frequently invite tai chi teachers to present a class for my music students because there is a profound connection between such disciplines as yoga, tai chi, aikido or karate and music—and that connection is one of motion, of movement.

Activity: Breath and Circle

I have already mentioned Chungliang Al Huang's technique of gathering the energy from the heavens, taking it into the body and then sending it out in a big circle—and when he first spoke to me about it I saw an immediate application to playing a string instrument. Just imagine that every movement includes a breath you take in and an infinitely large circle to which your energy goes out.

1. How do you place your bow on any string instrument?
2. Instead of picking it up and resting it on the string, bring it around in a circle as you inhale and draw the bow as you exhale.
3. When you release the bow, perhaps bring it up into the air in another circle.
4. What does that feel like?

Your own creativity can assist you in coming up with equivalent exercises for your instrument, or you can try one of the exercises that follow:

Activity: Imaginary Tai Chi Movement in Sound

1. Play Bach's well-known "Air on the G String" from his *Orchestral Suite No. 3*.
2. Listen only to the melody.
3. Allow your hands and arms to arch with the tempo at of the music.
4. Create a large, imaginary ball in the space in front of you with your arms and hands as you breathe in sympathy with the music.
5. When your hands reach the bottom of this imaginary ball, carry it around the room in slow motion in time with the music, slowly raising and lowering the ball in front of you and passing it around your body.
6. Gently rest the ball on the floor at the end of the music.

Reflection

1. Wasn't that amazing?
2. Listen to other kinds of slow, expressive music and imagine similar movements you would like to make to these pieces.
3. Are you able to transfer the speed of a pulse into an actual physical movement in your hands, arms or body?

I had the profound joy of watching David Darling play his cello to the amazing tai chi movements of Chungliang Al Huang at our 2005 Inspiration in Music workshop. It was the most perfect blend of movement and music I have ever seen. I attended another concert at which aikido masters performed their movements as an ensemble to the exciting music of Bach's *Brandenburg Concertos*—it was hard to imagine at the time that this music was written for any other purpose.

Activity: Tai Chi Pizzicato

1. Pluck the string of any string instrument to create one note that resonates for several beats.
2. As the string vibrates, exhale, making a large circle in the air with your hand.
3. Mentally expand the circle you make with your hand and body until it extends to the ends of the space you are playing in—to the far end of the room or out into the sky.

Reflection

1. What did it feel like to project your sound to the end of the space you occupy?
2. Can you deliver this sound to a space beyond the physical boundaries of the area you are actually sitting or standing in with your instrument—outside the room and into the heavens?

These tai chi sound and movement activities can be performed with any instrument. Imagine the cymbal player in a symphony orchestra. As the percussionist crashes cymbals together she opens them wide to release the vibration then brings them back around to her body, completing the circle. Watch another percussionist's movement as he uses a mallet or beater to strike a bass drum, triangle or the wood bar on a marimba. Watch a woodwind player as she plays one long note. Watch her body as she breathes in, then releases the note in the air. More than likely you will see a circle of movement.

Conductors of orchestras, bands and choirs use a circular gesture when they cut off a chord at the end of a piece.

Look for the tai chi circle!

If you have ever watched karate then you can probably visualize the power of a kick, the chop of a hand. Just think about the intensity, power and strength in these movements. Put that energy into the sound of the first movement of Beethoven's *Fifth Symphony* or the finale of Tchaikovsky's *Fifth! Boom!*

It's in taiko drumming (Japanese ensemble drumming) that music probably comes closest to the martial arts—the sound we hear is strongly enhanced by the tension and strength of its delivery through the body, through the stroke.

Watch for the flowing circle of energy that accompanies the drummers' movements!

One of my dear friends and bass colleagues, Diana Gannett, is not only a virtuoso bassist and professor at University of Michigan but a black belt in aikido. She and I have discussed the many benefits of aikido training as it relates to whole mind/body thinking. When I asked her how this relates to bass playing, she said,

Almost all musicians play from their brain, and the body just tags along. When you do that, the source of a player's movement is often in the smaller muscles instead of in the core of the body, and this can lead to all kinds of tensions and injuries. In aikido the body stays loose and relaxed, ready to respond from its core out.

Grounding

Diana's aikido training has taught her about grounding her body weight to help relax her upper body. Learning this kind of grounding alone can sometimes *double* a person's sound on the bass. Diana told me:

> When you play bass, there's a tendency to center your energy high in the body. We do this because it seems we must reach *over* the bass and then *press in* to play it—but this is an inefficient use of gravity, and why fight the most powerful physical force in our world? If we allow our weight to interact with the instrument instead of the using this press/push combination, it increases our sound as well as eliminating needless tensions.

In addition to grounding, aikido has taught Diana how to extend physical energy throughout the body and into the limbs. This is something that all musicians must do if they are to channel the music through their bodies and out to an audience.

Doesn't it all make you want to go out and do some musical tai chi, karate or aikido? I propose that the study of *any* martial art will have a direct impact on your integration of energy, balance, strength and spirit as you use your body for artistic expression.

Nia—a Wonderful Discipline with Many Musical Benefits

Nia is a personal-growth body-mind-spirit fitness program that you can find in most cities throughout the United States and abroad. It is a system that works with the natural wisdom and intelligence of the body, mind, spirit and emotions. Nia blends a range of rhythmic music styles with carefully choreographed hour-long movement routines. It is a "fusion fitness" program inspired by three major disciplines: the dance arts—including Jazz, Modern and Isadora Duncan; the healing arts—specifically yoga, Feldenkrais and the Alexander Technique; and the martial arts—aikido, tae kwon do, and tai chi.

My violinist friend Patricia Miner turned me on to Nia while we were colleagues playing together in the California Symphony Orchestra in 2005 when she took our Inspiration in Music class. She told me that Nia was one of the most meaningful physical disciplines she had done and described the great impact it had on her violin playing and teaching. This really interested me, and when I realized that Danielle Woermann, the mother of one of my most outstanding bass students, is a black-belt Nia instructor in the Bay Area and even taught classes in my own community, I had to check this out. Boy, was I glad I did!

Most people take Nia classes for the fitness and general feeling of well-being it delivers. A Nia class usually takes place in an exercise facility such as a dance or yoga studio. It brings terrific spirit into class through the great diversity of its instructors, the wide range of popular and world music it uses with its routines and the joy and freedom that are an essential part of every session. Certified teachers lead these mostly choreographed classes, but there is also room for improvisation in almost every class. Everyone can participate at their own pace and nobody gets hurt!

I have taken several of Danielle's Nia classes. I enjoyed the sessions so much that I asked Danielle to design some classes that helped bass players connect their body movements to specific rhythmic and melodic elements in music. Now Danielle is teaching Nia at my Golden Gate Bass Camp. I have personally been inspired by the opening of physical channels to parts of my body that I had no idea could move to music! It sounds strange to say this, but I have found new connections to my feet, legs, buttocks, stomach, chest, shoulders, arms, hands, neck and head—they are now more alive and help me connect to my bass in a deeper, more satisfying way!

My violin colleague Patricia had the privilege of studying with Carlos Rosa, one of the two founders of Nia when he was teaching in Marin County, California. I asked her about her experiences and she told me she loved the fact that she was free to vocalize and improvise while moving within the class structure.

Nia has the ability to ground you in your body thus bringing a new awareness of your energy and connecting you to your center...what the Japanese call *hara*. My workouts consisted of a spectrum of movements drawn from tai chi, aikido, yoga, and dance, creatively integrated together into one routine. As a classically trained violinist the most liberating part of the class was when I was asked to bring my awareness to one thing, whether it was feeling the sensation of my bare feet touching the earth, or finding joy in my movement.

As classical musicians we learn to develop and perform from our small muscles, yet it actually is our big muscles and our core that give us strength and flexibility. Nia allowed me to wake up to these areas in my body and use them to play with more ease and physical energy. I once asked Carlos how to prepare for a big audition and his response was to wear a belt around my waist that was large enough where I could be aware of my breath moving in and out from that area, and then the music flowing from the breath.

As classical musicians we are trained to observe the conductor for our artistic inspiration and learn to play from a hundred-year-old tradition that was developed from someone else's body. Nia brought me back to what was natural and right for my own body, as it is today. I learned how to look within and honor my own creative inspiration, in the different forms which it manifests as a teacher, and musician.

Jeanne Jackson is a white-belt Nia teacher in Charlottesville, Virginia, who has applied her Nia experience to her professional piano teaching. She wrote to me:

I adore Nia! It's what my body and soul crave. Ever since I stepped into my first Nia class, I have felt the healing power of Nia in my life. I am an independent music teacher with a sizable class of piano students. I immediately began using Nia techniques.

I noticed that my second student of the day, a ninth-grade girl, slumped her shoulders while sitting on the piano bench. Without mentioning her posture, I asked if she could sense her bare feet on the floor and her bottom on the piano bench. Using the Nia technique of connecting with sensation worked instantly—she immediately drew her spine up in the most graceful, flamingo-like manner. Amazing!

InterPlay Allows for a Free Improvisation Exploration of the Body, Mind and Spirit

InterPlay is an active, creative way to unlock the wisdom of your body. InterPlay founders Cynthia Winton-Henry and Phil Porter have trained over 200 teachers, conducting classes in most states in the United States and many foreign countries. InterPlay's international headquarters is in my hometown of Oakland, California, and I was introduced to their program through my wife Mary who studied InterPlay as part of her masters degree in Culture and Spirituality at Holy Names University (also in Oakland). I found these classes to be remarkably helpful for musicians.

InterPlay allows you to explore feelings and movements through your body on several levels. After a well-organized body warm-up that includes massaging the face and voice, you are left free to move around the room to inspiring music. There is an opportunity to quiet the mind by allowing the worries and daily concerns you carry around with you as tensions in the body to be expressed—leaving you free and in the moment. You are allowed to make eye or body contact with others in the room, or to go in your own private direction.

Cynthia Winton-Henry believes the body doesn't stop at the skin but extends to include a world body spirit beyond the physical being—and thus includes others who enter our space. Something akin to this is certainly true for musicians, who must share their inspiration with an ensemble by joining their expression with the expressions of others as it is sent out into the world.

Cynthia told me:

Moving is not the only thing bodies want to do. They want to breathe, to give voice, to create characters—and to interact. These are the four principles of InterPlay:

movement, voice, story and stillness. Our bodies want to move and breathe and find ways to express themselves in community through music, dance and storytelling.

Attending InterPlay allowed me to open very natural connections to my body through my breath and also through words, stories and improvisation.

> When we start moving and breathing, people often begin to tone or sing along quite naturally. When you do a thrusting movement like in a karate chop or kung fu kick, you may say "hey!" or "pow!" quite naturally—the movement awakens the body, and the voice follows. And breathing helps you come back into your body.

Another exercise involves telling a story with the hands in a kind of sign language. First tell the story with hands and no words, then repeat the exercise with both words and hands. Once again, this provides a way to express feelings and emotions with the body first, not words.

Activity: Put the Feelings in Your Body

1. Put on a piece of music in any style you'd like.
2. Use just one hand to express the energy and spirit-pulse-feeling of the music at every moment.
3. Play the music again, this time with your hands behind your back.
4. Move your shoulders, chest, stomach and hips as you previously moved your hand to express the energy, pulse and feelings in the music.

5. Now hold your hands as if you were playing a musical instrument.

6. Allow your body to continue to move as you play your imaginary instrument.

Reflection

1. Did you listen to the music in a different way, so as to bring the feelings in the music inside you—so you could move your hand?

2. How did you notice your breathing change while you were moving your body?

3. Was it different when you moved your body instead of your hand? More intense? More confined?

4. How did you body move while playing an imaginary instrument?

5. Did you feel like singing along with the music as you played the imaginary instrument?

Patricia Plude, a distinguished pianist, educator, interdisciplinary artist and Director of the San Francisco Walden School Teacher Training Institute has been associated with InterPlay and their professional dance ensemble Wing It! She told me that prior to meeting Cynthia and Phil she felt trapped by her conservatory training—she felt it was so focused on the printed page and the proper execution of notes and rhythms. I feel we so often get bound in our own disciplines. We learn too much, and then we can no longer approach our art with playfulness and a child's eye, and the freedom to just do it. I had to come back to music through the back door, through dance and storytelling. We start with storytelling first because words are easier for people to access.

Here is an example of one such exercise:

Activity: Three-sentence Story

1. Stand in a small circle of three-to-five people (or do this alone).
2. Go around the circle quickly, each person saying, "I could tell a story about..._____" (fill in the blank with a short, topical phrase or sentence).
3. First focus on something that happened to you in the last twenty-four hours.
4. Repeat the process with something that happened:
    a. in the last week,
    b. in the last month,
    c. in the last year.
5. Choose one of the topics mentioned.
6. Go around the circle again, asking each person to tell a short story in just three sentences with a beginning, middle and end.
7. Now stand in a circle (or alone) with your instrument or voice.
8. Go around the circle quickly, each person improvising a short snippet of music.
9. Approach this little musical phrase with the same abandon with which you said, "I could tell a story about _____," or "I can play *this*...!"

2. Move from the short, "I can play this…" phrases into three-sentence musical stories, each person improvising beginning, middle and closing phrases—a complete, miniature musical composition.

Reflection

1. How did approaching musical improvisation from the starting place of storytelling feel?
2. How did the "I can play this…" exercise feel?
3. How did the concept of a "three-sentence story" feel in storytelling?
4. How did it feel to transfer it to your instrument?

When music is spontaneous and unpredictable it is more interesting and really comes to life. Any movement, drama, story or singing that inspires you to recapture your playful side is a legitimate approach to your art. Discover what captures your childlike enthusiasm and passion and make that your pathway to finding the life in music!

Teaching Dances through the Body not the Mind: Just Do It!

Masankho Banda is a native of Malawi, Africa, an international peace-builder, educator and InterPlay leader who lives in Oakland, California. He taught me a powerful lesson about learning movement.

I tell my dance students: bring your body into the dance studio and *leave your head at the door*! I tell them, If you bring your head in with you, you will spend the next sixty minutes saying, "Yes, that's right, no, that's wrong."

I say, Trust your body. If you want to teach your body something, why on earth would you need your mind to tell your body what to do? Why don't you just let your body learn what it needs to know—it has its own way of learning!

I learned the same lesson sitting in a drum circle trying to pick up drumming patterns: the more I think, the worse it gets—but when I just relax, listen and let my hands move in sympathy with the group, it works much better!

Masankho told me a story about how the body has to abstract knowledge from past physical experiences of doing familiar things—gestures and movements that are natural.

I took forty Americans to my father's cottage in my hometown in Malawi, to teach my guests how to dance. And you know, it wasn't until we started the class that I realized this business of teaching people to dance was completely foreign to my native villagers—how could they teach someone how to dance, when they themselves had never been taught?

In my village, if there's a harvest dance or a wedding dance, everyone already knows the dances. We have been surrounded by music, drums, songs, and dancing since we were first able to crawl, and when one of us joins a dance, it's a dance they have been seeing since they were children. All they have to do is join in.

Masankho explained that the only way his American friends could learn the movements was for the Africans to slow it down so the newcomers could copy it a little at a time. They watched and then did it themselves. They couldn't put numbers and steps to the movements; it wasn't something you'd notate or think about and remember that way. They just had to do it! African music is based on call-and-response—the leader calls, the group responds. So there's nothing to memorize.

Masankho also makes use of familiar imagery that is encoded in our body experiences as a way to bridge the gap between student and teacher and also avoid intellectual processing.

> You don't teach dance—we already know this. What we need to do is to find a natural way to express it. I tell them, "Your legs are *kissing* the earth!" You understand the concept of kissing, I'm sure! That's my code for bringing this dance step into my body—I call it the *kiss*.

> There is a song known as *A Call to the Ancestors*. I ask, "Where would you want your ancestors to be within your body?" In your *heart*, of course! So instead of thinking, "Step, reach, pull, down," think of bringing the ancestors into your heart!

> There is an immediate, kinesthetic, familiar relationship established between what we are learning and an *internal* motion that we already want to make. *We are all singers, waiting to sing, dancers waiting to dance, and musicians waiting to play.*

Focusing on Your Core Source of Energy Using Gravity

I met Fanchon Shur while playing with the Cincinnati Symphony Orchestra. She was teaching a program called Growth in Motion that attracted musicians of many cultures, and I found that her work is consistent with the tai chi principle of embodying energy that comes from the earth, passes through the body and out into the world. Much of Fanchon's bodywork continues the traditions and principal teachings of Body-Mind Centering by Bonnie Bainbridge Cohen, Rudolph Laban and Irmegard Bartenieff as well as the Feldenkrais principles. Fanchon told me:

> You have to drop down from your thinking brain into your chi center at the navel, entering the place where you were unconditionally nourished in the womb. Everything spreads out from there.

> I do this work on the floor. Before you can stand or sit, you need to be able to surrender to gravity, and allow your contact with the earth to help you reach out with lightness.

Activity: Breathing from the Floor

1. Lie on your back on the floor, with one hand gently fusing with the lower ribs where your lungs begin.
2. Place your other hand on your chest, under your collarbone.
3. Notice your breath. It starts in the lower abdomen and ends in the upper chest under the collarbone.
4. On the exhale the breath leaves the higher place and goes to the lower.

Fanchon believes there is a connection from the center of our body, through our legs and feet, to the center of the earth that also radiates infinitely outwards. When we imagine our connection beyond the floor to the center of the earth we connect with an energetic flow that feeds our expansiveness and empowers our musical energy as it goes out into the world.

Activity

1. Lie down.
2. Put your hand on your navel.
3. Envision yourself unconditionally fed, nourished and loved.
4. Imagine your navel creating a warm, loving "lava flow" which spreads to another part of your body.
5. Move your hands along this imaginary flow.
6. Is every part of the body connected to your center?
7. Move your awareness from the center to different parts of the body.
8. Feel the flow of energy in your blood stream as it enters your arms and hands.
9. Try the same exercise with your breath. Feel it carrying energy from your center to the periphery and back.
10. Let the flow of energy radiate from your navel center to your muscles.
11. Feel the energy radiate through your muscles from your center to your extremities and back again.
12. Do you feel a different quality of movement when you visualize your muscles passing the energy along as opposed to your bloodstream or your breath?

13. Allow the energy from your center to move through the nervous system.
    a. Allow its sensitive alertness to emanate from your spinal cord and radiate through your nerves into every part of your body, even your skin.
    b. This is a different kind of energy than that carried via your breathing, bloodstream or muscles.
14. Feel the fluid in every joint in your body; just put your awareness there.
15. Feel the flexibility of the fluids in your shoulder, elbow, wrist and finger joints, your knee, ankle and toe joints, as you move your body.
16. Create a relationship with gravity.
17. Yield your body to the earth.
18. Start pushing into the earth.
19. When you push into the earth, allow one part of your body to elevate while another part is connected to the earth.
20. When you use the power of gravity it frees your upper body to elevate: wherever you push, there is another part of you that can lift and reach.

Fanchon explained that extending the body without negotiating with gravity produces a tight quality that doesn't work. But yield into the power of the earth first, and you can use all that power. This allows you to be "strong with gravity and light in defying it." When you push the right side it frees the left side of the body; when you push with both legs, you free the upper body to reach out and go somewhere. And when you play an instrument, first yield into and then push against gravity—to liberate your arms, fingers and upper body to be free and expressive. This body and energy exercise allows an artist to connect with the core, where all the power and strength resides.

There is a qualitative difference between the movements of our body and the sound of our music when we use the pull of gravity and harness the flexibility in the fluids in our joints. The percussionist uses gravity instead of hitting, and string bowing becomes more flexible in the wrist.

Movement and Music—the Integration of the Two

I have been collaborating with movement specialist, choreographer and dancer Alan Scofield for thirteen years, exploring ways to help musicians connect with body and movement while holding violins, flutes and basses in their hands. Our work includes first encouraging students to make appropriate stylistic body movements that capture the spirit and character of the music—dance—then helping them combine these movements while holding instruments in their hands or mouths.

Alan reminds me:

We move our audiences the way the music first moves us. So the musician's emotions must be fully available to the music—but since the body is much more intelligent than the conceptual mind, there has to be an emotional, kinesthetic response. The body is supremely intelligent in terms of guiding itself within a musical flow, but one has to surrender completely to the music.

Alan has the gift of connecting body movements to feelings, sounds and words. In working with a few outstanding orchestras in the San Francisco Bay Area he has created an environment where self-conscious students who might normally be reluctant to dance to music can surrender at once to the musical spirit and respond spontaneously with the most natural body movements. He employs the African tradition of call-and-response to keep the task simple and his students in a non-thinking, imitative state, engaging them in improvisational movement with plenty of freedom for self-expression.

So much music—from Bach to hip hop—is based on dance forms. Our goal is to keep the dance alive while playing the right notes, rhythms and bowings on our string instruments. But it can be difficult to get high school musicians to actually dance while they play their violins and basses—even though we expect to see just that when we hear the Kronos String Quartet!

At the 2008 Golden Gate Bass Camp Alan and I coached an ensemble of four basses in a minuet by Bach. It was wonderful to have Alan teach the students to do this Baroque dance while holding their basses in the left hand without playing. When we asked them to play and dance at the same time, though, their bodies froze—and they just played the notes as before. It was too difficult for them to co-ordinate dance movement with bowing and fingering notes. No problem! We simplified the task, asking them to just dance in their shoes!—and voila—they found they could easily shift their weight to the minuet steps while keeping their feet planted on the floor. We combined the dance with the music and the notes jumped right off the page!

In our daily Bass Camp movement class Alan gave us another exercise that combined words with body expression. Alan found some powerful phrases in Walt Whitman's *Leaves of Grass*, and we had students say the words while a demonstrating a body gesture—much like they would in the game of Charades.

Here is an example of the text.

> The *winds...blowing,*
> The boy...*ecstatic,*
> With his bare *feet*...in the *waves...*
> The *love*...in the *heart*...long *pent*...now *loose...*
> *Now*...at *last...tumultuously...bursting...*

> Think of a gesture for *winds,* such as the arms lifting or waving
> *blowing*—spreading the hands from the face away from the body
> *ecstatic!*—jumping and reaching up
> *feet...the waves...*—what do you do here?
> *Love*—a gesture toward the heart, and the tone of voice!

This exercise helped students create *meaning* with their body gestures. Now we had to translate that meaning in words into the meaning of a note or phrase of music...

Activity: Embody Words, Feelings and Sounds

With each of the following words:

1. Think of the word.
2. Take a deep breath.
3. As you exhale, make a *movement* with your arms, legs, body—like a conductor or dancer—that expresses the *feeling* of the word.
    a. Don't *say* the word.
    b. Just show the feeling of the word with your body gesture.

- Exhale *joy*
- Exhale *suspense*
- Exhale *beauty*
- Exhale *anxiety*

4. This time add the sound of *one* or *two* notes to coincide with the syllables of the word.

   a. They can be any two notes in the character of the feeling, but with a *full body delivery*!

   b. Say *Joy* (one note only) or *Suspense* (two notes).

   c. Let your body express joy with animated arms and facial expression.

   d. Lift up with your legs as you make a joyous sound on your instrument—just the one note.

5. Repeat this exercise with the other words above or invent your own words and sounds.

This opens the body to movements that are based on *meanings and feelings* of words. Now we must add feeling and meaning to the music we play. Every phrase has a *character* that can be expressed via the energy and movement of the body, but this requires us to have a clear understanding of the feeling in the music if we want to transmit it via the body to others.

This exercise is one of the most powerful steps we can take toward opening the physical channels that can allow us to express the elegance of Mozart—or the celebration in Jimmy Hendrix!

Movement Rules!

In the Spring of 2008, Alan Scofield played a piece called *Cannot See His Color* from James Howard's score for M. Night Shyamalan's movie *The Village*. He instructed the Lowell High School Orchestra players to move around the room without their instruments, allowing their arms and bodies to express the eloquently flowing violin lines played by Hilary Hahn. The students moved as though they were playing the violin, conducting an orchestra, or flapping their wings in the air like butterflies or birds—it was a beautiful sight.

Next, Alan asked them to confine their movement to a radius of a few feet. Then he asked them *not* to move their feet to the music, but only their legs, hips, and arms. After that, he told them to pretend they were holding and bowing their instruments (violins, cellos or basses) while still moving their bodies to the soundtrack. They only had to air-bow their instruments and dance! Finally, we asked them to improvise and imitate the notes on the CD while continuing their body movement.

We made it clear that the music was to be inspired by the feelings in their bodies and the movements that flowed from those feelings! What a profound sound we all made—we were tapping directly into inspiration and allowing the spirit of the music to control our playing.

And this isn't—or shouldn't be—something special. This is the way music is usually performed by the greatest of artists.

I have never experienced such a transformation in sound as I heard that day. And that same exercise could be repeated with the music of Beethoven, Brahms or with any ensemble music played by an orchestra, band or choir. The movement of the musicians is the primary exercise, and they must draw their inspiration directly from the spirit of the music itself. In fact, playing with instruments right at the end is the *least* important part of the exercise.

When the inspiration comes *first* through the body—rather than from the printed page or the brain—you will really notice the difference—I assure you. The music springs to life immediately.

I invite you to discover your own unique movement discipline for making deeper connections to your body and nurturing them. It may be ballroom dancing, karate, contact improvisation or yoga—the form of movement doesn't matter; it's the movement itself that counts. Movement is our primary way of expressing ourselves.

I close this chapter with the words of Deborah Bull, dancer, writer and Creative Director of the Royal Opera House in London, who very wisely said:

> Body language is a very powerful tool. We had body language before we had speech, and apparently 80% of what you understand in a conversation is read through the body, not the words.

I'm convinced that if you watch any great artist who is making music come alive you will see physical energy and body movement. Movement taps directly into heart and soul. The performer's body speaks directly to the listener's body, and has the power to move us on many levels.

And it is never too late to unlock the wisdom of the body. The Greek historian Xenophon tells the story of Socrates learning to dance when he was already an old man because he felt he had neglected an essential part of his being up to that point. Don't neglect your body. Love it, nurture it, train it, move it, groove it, feed it—but most importantly, use it! And then let Mozart dance through you!

Part III
Inspiration

Chapter 7
The Complete Package

There are no guarantees in bringing music to life.

It may catch you by surprise, you can be prepared for it, but there are no absolute guarantees. All creativity is like that. Even Beethoven had days when his musical ideas just weren't that interesting, and Einstein had his problems with math. He once told a graduate student, "Don't worry, my math problems are far worse than yours." But the Einsteins and Beethovens still achieve wonders, because they are prepared, and because they give themselves to the task with passion.

So there may be no guarantees in bringing music to life, but it's possible—and worth doing with preparation and passion.

In Part I we identified the three elements that contribute to bringing music to life: Breath, Pulse and Movement; in Part II we discussed how to master each. Now in Part III, dedicated to inspiration, we hope that the balance and integration of these elements will produce the conditions for something special to happen. I say "we hope" because that something special cannot be forced or manipulated.

It cannot be guaranteed. It cannot be controlled.

Balance and Integration

The "complete package" is one in which Breath, Pulse and Movement are balanced and integrated. They are balanced when all three have been given proper attention, when we are at ease with our Breath, Pulse and Movement. And they are integrated when they work together as a single stream, in a single flow of energy.

In computer-speak, that is called multitasking.

I am talking about the *simultaneous* integration of Breath, Pulse and Movement in one non-thinking and non-controlling state. This is really a matter of allowing the *body* to do its thing! On one level this is remarkably complex. It requires practicing and then mastering these individual elements to the point where you don't have to think about them, you just do it! And when that happens, it's like a surfer effortlessly riding a wave! At that magical moment the surfer dissolves into the wave; wave and surfer become one.

This is our goal: for both performer and audience to dissolve into the spirit and life in the music, to ride the wave!

I'd like you to indulge me with an exercise that uses technology so you can get the full impact of this "complete package." I want you to go to a computer if possible and watch some short YouTube clips. I have chosen five specific videos that show musicians performing which help translate what we have been talking about into sound, sight—and inspiration. If you don't have access to the internet, you can still read the text and *imagine* the musician's performances. But I assure you that if you take time to watch these five short videos, my words will really come alive for you and it will be easier for you to recognize the importance of our three principles and be inspired by the "complete package" once you've seen these things in action!

These pictures are worth more than the 5,000 words in this chapter!

And I've added a sixth video, too. It's not about music—but I'll keep that one secret for now.

> **Note:** YouTube internet addresses often change over time or become obsolete. If the following addresses do not work, search YouTube for the artist and/or title of the composition.

Joshua Bell Plays Debussy

http://www.youtube.com/watch?v=G4Xgxdulv_0 (2:28)

We begin with music that reaches the soul—and contains all the elements you might associate with energetic, fast-moving, lively music. Joshua Bell is one of my favorite musicians. He is not only one of the greatest violinists of our time, but he elevates his audiences with him into a sacred space. My interview with Joshua was one of the most powerful and profound of those I conducted for my book, *The Mastery of Music*. He described "surrendering to the spirit of Beethoven" with such grace and real humility.

Watch "Joshua Bell playing *The Girl with Flaxen Hair* by Debussy" with the Orpheus Chamber Orchestra (the link is above). You can see him communing with the spirit of the music. It's there in the position of his raised head, his unfocused eyes, the way his mouth is open as if he is singing and playing at the same time. His elegant body movement relays the essence of the music as he moves in time to the pulse. With almost every beat (about once a second), Bell shifts body position as if to reflect the surging emotions in the music. His heart is open. His breath is the embodiment of feelings of love, beauty, grace, gratitude, spontaneity and passion, with fleeting movements of tenderness, peace and ecstasy. He has gone beyond just "performing" the music to embodying its essence.

You can see the gentle flow of the pulse, too, in the body movements of the Orpheus Chamber Orchestra: the pulse is flexible, spontaneous and alive—it is in the moment.

I invite you to role-play Joshua Bell playing the violin. After you have viewed the video at least twice, watching with care Joshua's movements, his amazing playing and profound spirit, I want you to join him. Here's how:

Activity: Play the Role of Joshua Bell

As you replay the video clip, imagine you are Joshua Bell.

1. *Breath.*
   a. Allow your breath (or half-whistle) to play along with the rhythm of the notes in the melody.
   b. Play the melody for Joshua Bell while you breathe in and out, expelling each breath as though you are whistling.
   c. Or you can *groan* along with the melody, not attempting to copy the pitches, using your vocal chords in the rhythm of the melody.
   d. Or you can sing along, if you are comfortable actually matching the melody of the violin.
   e. Breathe in the feeling of love and tenderness.
   f. As you sing or exhale, express these same feelings.
2. *Pulse.*
   a. Notice the slower quarter-note pulse in the harmony.
   b. The primary rhythm of the melody is a long note followed by two shorter notes.
   c. There is a flowing pulse made up of four sixteenth notes for every quarter note (with variations).
3. *Movement.*
   a. Watch Joshua's body movements.

    b. Begin by shifting your weight, twisting or swaying back and forth with your shoulders.

    c. Then allow this movement in your hips.

    d. Perhaps you see him moving up or down.

    e. Now focus on your arms as you and Joshua together move with the music.

    f. Finally, notice how you can shift the position of your head.

    g. Enjoy yourself. Relax, and give yourself to the music.

4. Imitate different body movements until you don't have to think about what you are doing. You're just swinging along with the master, with the spirit of the music.

5. While you are breathing along with the music, include the pulse with your swaying body movement.

6. Pretend you are holding the violin in your hand as you sing.

7. Bow and move to the music.

Reflection

1. What did you notice when you internalized the feelings of beauty in the music with your voice?

2. How did you feel when the pulse became flexible?

3. What emotions did you feel in your body?

4. What did you feel in your legs and abdomen? in your heart? in your head?

5. Did you want to close your eyes?

The music becomes real when it embraces not just the one element of breath but when the body engages Breath, Pulse and Movement at the same time. And for the body to be free to move and express itself in this way you have to know the music so well that you are no longer preoccupied with technique.

No one said this was easy—that's why we practice. We want to train the mind and body to work without effort or deliberate control so we can just feel the music and express it through the body—without thinking!

Kronos Quartet—Foxy Lady!

http://www.youtube.com/watch?v=ja35dyPxE74 (3:20)
Rock music is all about energy and the groove! But where do we feel the groove?

Thanks to YouTube, you can still catch Jimi Hendrix himself playing *Foxy Lady* (http://www.youtube.com/watch?v=hb7ln5vlS_k), but what I'd like you to do now is to watch the phenomenal twenty-first century Kronos String Quartet playing Hendrix' song (the link is above). You'll see how the integration of Breath, Pulse and Movement transforms the quartet into one giant Hendrix-machine, inspiring the listener to move and sing along.

The quartet's intense physical energy captures the spirit of *Foxy Lady*—and this same intensity can be present whether you're playing Mozart, Beethoven or Brubeck. Watch carefully to see how the players' body movements relate to the sounds of the violins, viola and cello. It all starts with the groove shared by the cellist, Jennifer Culp, and two violinists, David Harrington and John Sherba. What we are really seeing and hearing here is three string players taking the part of a rock drum beat. That's right. It's three string players becoming bass drum, cymbals and drums in full throttle!

The cellist shows the pulse with her head, but her body really moves from its core. I feel sorry for the strings on the cello! Check out the body movements of the violinists as their bows hit the strings. Their strumming pizzicatos vibrate the strings like sticks crashing a ride cymbal! It's awesome! The rhythm of the groove prepares for the melody.

Observe the violist (in the orange coat), Hank Dutt, who plays the melody before violinist Harrington takes it. Remember Joshua Bell playing his melody almost as though he was singing? You can see the same inner voice screaming out of Dutt. His breath sustains the powerful sound of his viola. If you were to imitate the force and quality of this melody with your voice, you would probably half growl and push with your gut in a true rock manner! Now watch the other violinists play their melody. It's as if they are actually screaming with their violins. It's *breath*!

Play the clip again, and this time let's marvel at the sheer body energy each musician brings to this performance. Check out the intensity. Watch the violinists' pizzicatos—it's tai chi and karate! Look for the tai chi circle as the hand strikes the strings and recycles. Can you feel the sheer force that's transmitted through that violin? Here is where breath and body movement come together—*hooh*! *bam*! *wack*! Watch Herrington's body as he plays the melodic lines. When the line goes up, his body goes up—when it goes down, his body goes down. Which comes first? I say *the body*! Look at the *core* of the body of every one of these great musicians—and remember, the core is closest to the heartbeat and the groove!

If you danced to this music, you would want your body weight close to the ground. You would move from your center, from *hara*—connecting with the earth, and the Force would be with you.

The Kronos Quartet is creating every note *with their bodies!* Can you see the energy?

Now turn off the sound and just watch the musicians' movements as you play the clip again. Can you hear the music without the sound? Notice the speed of their movements between some of the notes—or after a note ends. Notice the confidence, intensity and strength of their judo! Can you see how practicing martial arts will help you play Jimi Hendrix?

Activity: Capture the Movement!

1. Turn off the sound and play the video.
2. Make tai chi circles with your hands as you see the players strike their strings.
3. Stomp your feet with the pulse as you see their heads move.
4. Imitate all the head movements—down, up, and sideways! *Don't hurt yourself!*
5. Pretend you are holding a violin and imitate the violinist's movements!
6. Create your own karate movements with your arms, forearms, kicking and punching in rhythm with the musicians on the video.

Reflection

1. When you saw the video without sound, what did you notice about the musicians' movements?
2. When you did the karate movements, what sounds did you make with your voice?
3. What vocal sounds did you make when you were grooving to the rhythm?

This *Foxy Lady* video gives us an example of two or three musicians sharing the rhythmic pulse while another musician plays a melody.

If you watch the violist carefully you can see his body moving to the pulse of his fellow musicians while he himself is playing a melody—a fine example of what I mean by the necessary multitasking that involves each person not only playing his own part but also engaging the body with the rest of the music. This is the "complete package" in action!

Tito Puente "El Rey del Timbal" Trio de Timbales

http://www.youtube.com/watch?v=CM5GPXU_-IE (4:27)

This YouTube video brings us a joyful, electrifying performance by the world-famous Latin percussionists Tito Puente, Sheila E and Pete Escovedo playing six timbales in front of a big band! It is a great example of three players sharing the groove between them, playing together as one, using their bodies to dance, celebrate, and march around in a circle as they alternate drumming solos—with Sheila at one point whirling her drumstick around her head like a lariat at a rodeo!

Tito Puente's facial expressions and breathing are the most animated. His head bobs up and down with delight and celebration as though he's slowly but surely moving into ecstasy, and his smiles and expressive eyes radiate his excitement. He sings along with the band's screaming trumpets as he embodies the spirit of every resonant sound! Sheila E smiles and glows with joy as she moves her body with every beat. As you watch this video it grabs your energy, inspires you to tap your feet, and makes you want to jump up and join in the fun!

Latin music is infectious—the congas, timbales, bongos and hand percussion instruments are at the center of every band. Last year I heard Pete Escovedo's big band at Yoshi's Oakland Jazz House with Pete Senior plus his son, Pete Junior and daughter Sheila

E. The rhythm section fronts the big band while all the musicians stand and dance through every tune. And let me tell you—there's an inseparable connection between pulse, movement and singing along with these guys that grabs your breath and infuses you with energy.

While this performance of Latin-style music showcases the three elements of Breath, Pulse and Movement in a truly vivid manner, it is true in general that the popularity of Latin salsa or Cuban music relates directly to the way it's performed. Everyone in the band—percussionists, winds, brass—*lives* this music *through* their whole bodies, and the spirit and life reaches right out into the audience—it's inescapable.

And it's not just a matter of drums and colored lights—the technique by which that Latin spirit is transmitted is the same as the technique we saw in Joshua Bell's beautiful performance of the sensitive, tender music of Debussy.

The complete package.

The Maestro Is the Model of the Heart and Soul of Every Performer

I think of a symphony orchestra—and large concert bands and choirs, too—as a sort of amplified version of a single human being making music. The main difference as I see it is that in the case of an ensemble, there are many participants performing different roles that are performed by a single individual in the case of a solo pianist, singer or instrumentalist. In an orchestra or large ensemble, many individuals participate in melody, rhythm and harmony, but in the final analysis, who is in charge?

The most visible person (albeit usually with his or her back to the audience) is the conductor. I compare the conductor to the brain of the solo musician. The conductor's role is to shape the music, make decisions as to tempo, style and balance, and then communicate his sense of the music through his hands or baton to the many individual musicians who make the sounds. Great ensemble players become experts at reading the energy, style and intent of the maestro, and this allows the maestro, like a puppeteer, to pull the strings of the many musicians in the large ensemble, impressing his own musical style on the final product.

Most music lovers have attended either symphony, opera, choral or band concerts and are used to seeing a conductor lead a large group with baton and expressive body movements. It is beautiful to watch as a piece of music seems to move invisibly from the printed page to the mind of a conductor, through his or her gestures to the musicians and from their swaying and expressive bodies to the audience. And the conductor's role in this is the ultimate challenge in multitasking—as well as embodying Breath, Pulse and Movement. It is a job so complex that every part of the mind, body and soul has to be engaged.

Bernstein Conducts the Finale of Tchaikovsky's *Fifth Symphony*

http://www.youtube.com/watch?v=2pypUXtDgX0 (4:51)

I grew up in the sixties when the great dynamic maestro, Leonard Bernstein was the conductor of the New York Philharmonic Orchestra. His legendary series of educational concerts on PBS inspired millions to hear and enjoy music. Bernstein was a national hero and my primary inspiration for falling in love with music. The highlight of my Cincinnati Symphony orchestral career was a double whammy—not only playing under Bernstein as our guest conductor, but also attending a concert in the front row of the balcony as I watched Bernstein lead an all-Tchaikovsky concert with the New York Philharmonic.

You can see the maestro in his prime and glory by watching the YouTube clip of him conducting the Finale of Tchaikovsky's *Symphony No. 5* by following the link above.

When you watch Bernstein you see the complete package right there. Start with the breath—you can see him singing along, mouthing his feelings, expressing the spirit of the music with every inhale and exhale. If you watch his body, it is amazing to see how he subdivides the pulse among head, arms and baton, legs, feet, and even his face, mouth and hair! And Bernstein's body movements not only reflect the pulse, but also the expression and character of the music, embodied in his energy, intensity and gestures.

Just watching his face you can see expressions of: power, delight, enthusiasm, pain and determination as he pleads, coaxes, cajoles, pulls, cheers and churns, celebrating, encouraging, feeling contentment, dignity, power and strength, then blasting, slamming, galloping, racing, riding and chopping, exuding gratitude, bliss, joy and fulfillment. I'm running out of words to describe everything that he shows us through his gestures alone—all that to pass on the power of Tchaikovsky's music.

You may notice a difference between the intense energy maestro Bernstein gives off and the energy of the musicians playing under his direction. The individual players are mellower in their emotional and physical intensity than the maestro. Their hands and mouths are occupied playing their flutes, trumpets and violins. In the sixties it was common practice for the maestro to show most of the movement and energy. The eyes of the audience were mostly on this astonishingly colorful conductor as well. But in the concert halls of the twenty-first century you will often find more body movement among the players reflecting the energy that is flowing from the maestro on the podium. We live in a more visual culture and our performance practices have changed with the times.

Activity: Play the Role of Leonard Bernstein

1. Watch the YouTube video of Bernstein conducting the Finale of Tchaikovsky's *Fifth Symphony* at least twice.
2. While watching it a third time imitate Bernstein's facial gestures! Feel the qualities and energy expressed in his face, the joy, the excitement...
3. Watch it again, and this time imitate Bernstein's body movements. Watch his upper head positions, upper body, arms and legs!
4. Repeat steps 2 and 3, singing along with the melody or rhythm that you hear in the orchestra while moving your body and expressing your feelings in your face! Now you are expressing, moving, conducting and singing all at the same time. You are Leonard Bernstein! Go for it!

Reflection

1. What facial expressions were easiest for you to imitate?
2. What was the difference between the intensity of your imitation and that of Bernstein's performance?
3. What was the most challenging part of the multitasking in step 4: beating time, expressing, singing and managing the orchestra all at the same time?
4. As you were role-playing Bernstein what feelings did you have while singing, conducting and moving your body?
5. Was this fun? difficult? inspiring? helpful?

The Complete Package Calls on the Conductor Within

There has to be a conductor of some kind in every musician, dancer, actor or public speaker! And by embracing the conductor within we can allow our bodies to respond to stronger and more vivid direction. The only difference is that here *you*, the artist, have to express yourself in sound by following the cues of your own inner maestro—so you have to be both maestro and performer in one body! As you are singing, grooving and moving, you are multitasking on a grand scale—and this is the complete package we are striving for!

Gustavo Dudamel/SBYOV: Shostakovich *Symphony No. 10*, Movement 2: "Allegro"

http://www.youtube.com/watch?v=2ZbJOE9zNjw (4:01)

Until this past year, Leonard Bernstein was my all-time musical hero.

Today I have a new hero in the form of twenty-seven-year-old Venezuelan maestro Gustavo Dudamel, who has captured the imagination and adulation of the worldwide music community much as Bernstein did in the sixties. I have seen him conduct twice in San Francisco, both with the Venezuela Youth Orchestra and as guest conductor with the San Francisco Symphony.

The response of my symphony colleagues in the orchestras of Berlin, Vienna, London and throughout the United States has been unanimous: Dudamel is the most sensational and engaging figure in music to come along since Bernstein. He embodies in his music making everything that I have expressed in *Bringing Music to Life*. He is the very model of bringing music to life in a way that electrifies audiences and musicians alike.

Watch the YouTube video (the link is above). The amazing thing about this performance is the conductor's relationship with the orchestra. Bernstein appears to exceed the energy of the players while dominating them with his incredible personality and dynamic interpretations. Dudamel, on the other hand, finds a way to achieve similar musical results while merging with the orchestra as just one member of the ensemble.

Dudamel played violin in the orchestra for many years before becoming the conductor. He said in a recent BBC interview:

A good conductor needs to be more than a leader. I am part of the orchestra, I am not the maestro. And I think this is a special thing, that the musicians have the opportunity to be the leader of the orchestra. When you have the freedom to play, you make special music. The conductor needs to be more than a leader, you need to feel that you are only a bridge between the composer and the orchestra, and you have to have humility. I think this is the most important quality of a conductor.

In this Shostakovich performance, Dudamel shows us how musicians can play with the same intensity as their conductor. Watch their movement and notice the freedom each musician has. Unlike some orchestras in which all the violins play in perfect synchrony as one, in this orchestra we have individuals playing with their own spirit and the energy is almost overwhelming. Yet I can personally say that when I heard Dudamel conduct the San Francisco Symphony in the complete Stravinsky *Firebird Ballet,* I heard the soft, quiet movements of the music played with a shimmering beauty and breathlessness in complete contrast to the vibrant, almost strident energy of this piece by Shostakovich. The soft and the exciting music were equally profound and effused with spirit.

These two concerts with Gustavo Dudamel are the most moving, exciting and emotional concerts I have ever witnessed.

Dudamel Uses His Breath
to Keep the Music Flowing

Watch and listen to this performance of the Shostakovich. It seems Dudamel never closes his mouth—he is breathing, smiling, celebrating and coaxing energy, and the music comes alive in a way that's clearly related to the maestro's guidance and flow. The music prevails.

As you watch you'll see the cymbal crashes make perfect tai chi circles. Rhythmic subdivisions are everywhere. Even when the music is soft, Dudamel's mouth remains open and content. And at one moment near the end of the movement Dudamel purses his lips and blows as though he's joined his friends in the flute section and is playing the melody with them. It's the breath, always flowing, sustaining the life in the music.

Dudamel does an amazing job of coaxing energy from his players without personally dominating the music. When I saw Michael Tilson Thomas conduct the San Francisco Symphony I noticed a similar synchronization of energy and spirit in the body language of both conductor and musicians—especially the string section. I see a direct relationship between this presence of body energy and the aliveness and communication of the power of the music.

When I see a conductor expending all the energy while the musicians sit slouched in their chairs with feet crossed, their eyes buried in the music, and looking as though they could care less as they play the notes on the music stand, I find myself sitting across from them in the audience, wanting to assume a similar posture—

and that's *not* good! And I'm amazed, frustrated and discouraged whenever I observe this kind of body language, whether it's among high-school musicians in youth orchestras, regional professional orchestras, choirs or any other type of ensemble. You may even see this kind of disconnect between the energy of a conductor and the orchestral musicians under her or his baton in a concert by some of our most well-known professional orchestras!

I invite you to *notice* the involvement and physical energy that the leader of any ensemble extends to the musicians. Then I hope you will notice how much of that physical energy and direction is *mirrored* by the players in the group he or she is leading. The final part of this exploration is to *listen* to the music once you are aware of any discrepancy between those energies and notice how it impacts the music you are hearing.

Bringing Music to Life is about committing ourselves one hundred percent in every facet of our performance. It is a complex and delicate challenge, and even with the best of intentions there are still no guarantees—but when we add integrity and discipline to this template of Breath, Pulse and Movement we put ourselves in a position where wonderful things can happen.

Then we can just sit back and let it flow!

Martin Luther King, August 28, 1963: I Have a Dream

http://www.youtube.com/watch?v=PbUtL_0vAJk (17:28)

As I have said throughout *Bringing Music to Life*, musical performance has a great deal in common with other disciplines of communication, including public speaking, theater, pantomime and all the dance/movement forms. All these endeavors require the complete package of an engaged breath, free and open body movement and a pacing or flow that typically manifests itself in some kind of pulse or rhythm.

The public speaker is another model of the embodiment of human inspiration, and in bringing this chapter to a close I'd like to turn your attention to what is perhaps the most famous speech of recent history by inviting you to watch one last video clip on YouTube.

Martin Luther King delivered his "I Have a Dream" speech in Washington DC in August, 1963 on the steps of the Lincoln Memorial. Take a moment to review the last three minutes of this historic message of inspiration and hope (the link is above).

Without question, the words and content of this speech can stand alone as an historical expression of the state of prejudice in America and an inspiring dream of the future. This profound message, presented with King's great oratorical skills, makes this one of the most memorable speeches of the twentieth century. When I listen to this speech I cannot help but be moved emotionally and physically—but allow me to objectively analyze the classic delivery of King's inspired words.

His vocal delivery is much like a song. Listen to the range (the high and low pitches) of his voice near the end of his speech and compare them to the beginning. You will notice a close connection between the emotions at the end of his speech and the range and timber of his voice when compared with the beginning.

Notice the pulse. King has been speaking for seventeen and a half minutes at a steady rhythm with energetic vitality every time he utters the phrases "I have a dream" and "let freedom ring" right at the end of a paragraph. The steady and emphatic pacing of his words contains meditative power, inducing an almost trance-like state of attention in his listeners. There is a rhythmic flow that we simply cannot overlook. And you will notice that King gently moves his body back and forth as he turns his head from side to side. Toward the end of his speech he begins to use one hand, then both hands and finally his entire body to punctuate the intensity of his words.

The complete package I have been describing integrates Breath, Pulse and Movement. You can see this integration in Joshua Bell's elegant movements and uplifting melodies, the Kronos Quartet's electrifying performance of Jimi Hendrix, Tito Puente's impassioned drumming, or the great maestros conducting Tchaikovsky and Shostakovich. With the life and spirit coming from the core of our human body we can just as easily recognize this expression in the art of public speaking. King's verbal delivery and his command of breath, rhythm and movement all work together in the delivery of this great and inspiring sermon to the nation and the world.

Chapter 8
Being in the Moment—
It's *You!*

My favorite salad consists of Bibb lettuce, grapes, candied walnuts and feta or blue cheese tossed in a raspberry vinaigrette dressing. I love its clashes and subtle blends of taste and texture. There's the crunch of honey-coated walnuts accompanied by the juicy sweetness of the grapes balanced by the tang of the blue cheese in that sweet-and-sour raspberry vinegar dressing—and all this over the delicate texture of Bibb lettuce.

That's a recipe that has been refined over time until the various balances are just right—and when we have friends over for dinner and offer them a plate of salad to go along with the meal and the sparkling conversation they provide it's a salad to remember. It's a salad with melody, harmony and rhythm—for me, it sings!

We have been exploring the basic ingredients that really bring music to life—Breath, Pulse and Movement—and seeing how they need to work together to fit each unique style of music. But what we really need is the inspiration to create something fresh, unique and memorable and to spin it with a magic touch. The life in music, like my salad, needs a balanced combination—intensity mixed with discipline blended with the tang of freshness and creativity over the delicate texture of simplicity.

This is really my own way of saying *It's me! It's you! It's this very moment!* This music comes through me, body and soul, and now I am sending it back out into the world in my own way, with my own sound. Mozart and Beethoven were both deeply moved by love and beauty—but while these feelings may have felt similar to each great composer, each of them manifested it in terms of his own unique harmonic and rhythmic language.

You remember that Allaudin Mathieu talked about hot and cold music—hot being the kind that comes directly from your juices without any notation, and cold being the kind for which a composer writes a score and that is played as written. I have experienced cold music really coming alive on a number of occasions as a classical bass player, but I have to admit that I have been consistently blown away by how *often* these life-giving moments occur as a result of improvising. When I've been playing in the moment, improvising with the many simple tools and forms that David Darling has taught us at Music for People, finding the life in music has become the norm.

I have spent six years learning more and more about this mysterious business of bringing music to life and exploring ways to apply what I've learned in my everyday teaching and playing of classical and jazz music. And one thing I've learned is this: music can be full to the brim of that special liveliness whether it's scored or improvised, hot or cold—but we have to be alive, ourselves, to making music in the moment.

Music that's alive this moment is music that's pulsating with energy and spirit—and it communicates! So *this is our true goal*—being in the moment. You can play Mozart in the spirit of improvisation and it will be as fresh today as it was when Mozart himself first played it two hundreds years ago.

I'd like you to meet several of my colleagues as they share their unique in-the-moment experiences both in improvisation and traditional educational settings. First, though, let me emphasize again that *you* are unique: you have a special voice and way of expressing yourself. All of my friends and colleagues presented here have found their own voices. I hope you will be inspired by their very different styles of music making and the diverse ways they work at making music come to life.

You are the one who gets to choose your way. *You* are the one with the power to let the music flow through your nervous system. *You* can walk this path, striving for music that is alive and not set in stone. *You* are as natural, playful, and creative as anyone else. *You* and only you can say it and play it *your way!*

Jerry Panone: Getting to the Moment

Jerry Panone is the orchestra director of the San Francisco School of the Arts and also a professional percussionist/drummer. I have had the distinct pleasure of working with Jerry for thirteen years. During that time I have held several experimental clinics with his large ensembles, exploring the principles expressed in each of my books in turn: *The Inner Game of Music, The Mastery of Music* and now, *Bringing Music to Life*. And I have to tell you, working with Jerry is like preaching to the choir. In my clinics at his School for the Arts I have essentially been paraphrasing some of the principles Jerry already teaches his students. He says:

All the techniques you use to bring voice, pulse and movement to the classroom are ways of telling the kids— there are more ways to get at what's in your heart than you might think—and we need to use them. Every day life just has too many distractions and complications—so how do we get around them? What you are doing, Barry, is offering kids ways of breaking through structures and conventions that may be good at some level—but can also become obstacles to playing music.

Helen Wang talks about this sort of thing (see chapter 3) and mentions that when kids are playing Baroque or Classical music the emphasis is often on playing the right notes, dynamics and fingerings—not on feelings. The idea of making the music our own by expressing our emotions is really new to many of us. Most of us are just not comfortable putting ourselves out there and perhaps sticking out in the group.

Jerry suggested that there is something about adolescence that resists being self expressive. I have seen him lose patience with his kids when they are not connecting with the music. He says:

> There are times when I'm giving it everything I have, and the kids just don't seem to have any personal relationship with the music. When I'm conducting and I look up and someone is out to lunch, it just kills the energy of the entire rehearsal. We really work to be in the moment at every rehearsal. Of our time together, 99% is spent in rehearsal, and we can't wait till a concert that could be six months from now, for something we need to practice every day. If you play a phrase in this moment it's something beautiful and exciting. But if you can't make real music in your daily rehearsals, you are spinning your wheels and completely missing the point.

Last year, Jerry was rehearsing the School for the Arts orchestra for their part in Mathieu's *Heart, Soul and Stomp!* The piece has a complex score and he was having trouble getting the kids to take the piece seriously. They were resisting the vocal singing and playing the non-traditional string sounds that were supposed to express anxiety or joy apathetically. Jerry slammed down his baton and said to the kids:

> JP: All right that's enough. This is bullshit. I've had it with this attitude and your half-assed playing of this piece. I want you to repeat after me: "Bullshit!"

The kids looked rather shocked at first, but then sheepishly repeated "Bullshit."

Then Jerry firmly instructed them to say it again—louder!

At that point the kids really got into it, and gladly screamed "bullshit!" at the top of their lungs, followed by hysterical laughter.

Jerry told the kids:

> JP: Now that you got that out of your system, let's get your heads into this piece and go back to work. And, by the way, don't tell your parents what we just said...

Jerry uses the kinds of exercises that are used to train actors. The idea is to get you out of your ego with its cares and concerns and into the present—but it also has to do with committing to the role, script or score. It's about leaving who you are, what you do and how you look behind and becoming the essence of your musical role.

Jerry talks about visiting Wroclaw, Poland, where he had seen an accordion duo playing classical favorites, Bach organ pieces and the like, in an open-air downtown square in front of a church. And these musicians were completely into it.

It just blew me away. These two accordionists, Alexander Burdyug and Andrey Fesenko, were oblivious to everyone around them—but there was this beautiful, magical music coming from their instruments.

Our challenge is to go from just playing notes to making magic. Getting into the music. I really hope the kids will find the joy that's possible when you play that way—and that it will last them the rest of their lives.

So how *do* you make it come alive?

I don't believe playing music with poor musicianship and a bad attitude can ever convey a great musical experience just because you are reading Beethoven's magical notes. Classical music needs the same kind of performance as spontaneous improvised music to bring it to life. Cold music, as Mathieu calls it, works on the principle that you must believe in and commit to it as you recreate it—that's when it jumps of the printed page and becomes a living experience.

Jane Buttars: Improvisation: It's spontaneous. It's *Me!*

Jane Butters is a classically trained pianist, vocalist, dancer, educator, improviser and very, very creative musician who leads a program called Music from the Inside. She believes you can best connect with your inner voice through improvisational techniques. Jane studied improvisation as a discipline to help discover the inner voice, and went through the Music for People leadership program in which she learned, among other things, to make up her lesson plan, then throw it away and do what's needed in the moment!

She told me that improvisation has given her a way to relate to her music without anyone else getting in the way. No composer can tell her what notes to play; no teacher can tell her how to practice: improvisation has been her way to play, to be with her instrument (voice, piano or body) and be herself. She says:

It's just me! And that's a gift that has profoundly affected my own playing. Everything I do has to show this new spontaneous relationship with music. Now when I approach a classical piece, I do so with a different perspective—that of a co-composer. You see, many composers write by improvising until they hear what they like—it's a part of their compositional process. Now that I've improvised for myself, I have a deeper understanding of that process and a closer connection to the composer and the piece. This adds a totally new dimension to my interpretation.

I made a CD of improvisations, and performed an entire concert improvising with dance, cello, drum, voice and piano. I couldn't imagine doing such things had I not been to Music for People and received such tremendous encouragement to accept myself as a total musician.

Since I was classically trained, I had been focused on recreating the music of others, feeling bound by the many rules of notation and the traditions handed down by my teachers—but to be sitting at the piano and creating right there in the moment, so the music is coming directly from me—it feels so authentic.

It's only me. In a way, it feels scary, but it is also liberating. And I find my personal experience is augmented and intensified when I'm improvising with other people—the non-rational part of the activity puts me in a different world—out of my head and into my heart or soul. It's a spiritual experience. That dimension of spontaneity is a *high*…it's extremely pleasurable and very rewarding.

What Jane is describing is the spontaneity and enthusiasm she experiences when she's participating in improvisational music—*because she is free to express herself.* It's her! It's getting into her inner feelings by removing the limitations that she feels the rules and traditions of formal instruction and notation can bring. And she has also found ways to include improvisation and self-expression in her teaching and playing of classical music:

I started by leading improvisation sessions at our local arts council and adult school, making a musical element the focus for each session—silence, rhythm, listening, imitation. Using improvisation, I worked with a women's spirituality group to help release spontaneous emotional feelings, taught deep listening and toning to a choir, and rhythm patterns to a dance class. Instead of teaching scales, literature and sight reading, my focus was to be open to the person in front of me, and go for whatever would reach them. This was a tremendous exercise of being in the moment.

I began attracting students I never would have dreamed of teaching. Professional musicians came to me for rhythm coaching. Composers came to me for help writing their music down. I've had blind students, Alzheimer's pianists who could no longer read music. And not only have I had the reward of helping people I could not have helped before, I've also expanded my bag of improvisation tricks in the process.

If someone is having technical difficulty with a passage, I encourage them to improvise using a small part of it— explore it, get to know it better. If they are having a memory problem, it might be because they don't really know the harmonic progression—so we might play a simple version of that progression together and take turns improvising over it. They get a deeper understanding of the part they aren't hearing.

It's *you* again. When you find new, spontaneous ways of expressing yourself, you are bringing your life's energy to the moment. It is truly an improvisation. Mozart tells us he heard his music all in one moment, then wrote it down—so it was sudden, it bypassed the worrying mind—it was like an improvisation, and he just wrote it down.

Improvisation *is* the life in the music—regardless if it's composed in a classical style or created spontaneously in a moment of insight.

Heather Keller: Getting to the Magic Is about Listening to the Breath

I met Heather through Music for People. She's a gifted harpist and singer who works professionally as a therapeutic music specialist for a small non-profit organization called the Children's Cancer Association founded by the parent of a child who died of cancer. Heather brings comfort, joy and hope to families who are going through illness with their children, and she works through improvisation. She says:

I used to perform specific pieces of written music in the patients' rooms. Now, I just walk into the room and listen to the kids. I base my work on what's going on in that moment with that child—and what captures their imagination. And what has helped me make this immediate connection, I find, is to be more connected to my own breath while being more aware of their breath. Their breathing tells me so much about the condition they are in. Listening to the silence helps me to be myself, and also to connect with the patient. And patience plays a role here, too. I can wait to feel what is present, instead of trying to make something happen.

During staff meetings, I ask everyone to bring something from their desk that can make a sound, and we go around the room improvising with our office supplies! They found that they could communicate with each other by expressing themselves in rhythms and movements with staplers, rulers, pens, and paper clips! We also have done singing on just one note—but with the same "one" quality of sound. This vocal exercise is a reminder that all you have to do to be making music is make a sound. This skips right past our notions of "better" and "worse" and "I can" and "I can't" and allows everyone to have a musical experience.

Heather's focus is on being tuned in to her patients. Her sensitive and intuitive presence allows her to give each person the kind of support they need to feel better. And her reliance on following the breath and paying attention to the silence helps put her in touch with who she is and how she can spontaneously minister in the most conscious way.

Ron Kravitz: Let It Flow from Your Body

Ron Kravitz is a percussionist, singer and master improviser, and another long-time graduate of the Music for People program. I played with Ron at one of my first jams at the Art of Improvisation Workshop in 2005 and was overwhelmed both by his musicianship and his way of expressing himself in music through his body. Later I found out that Ron attends weekly movement sessions in his home town of Philadelphia with an organization called Group Motion, where he doubles as a percussionist in the improvisation ensemble while also taking to the dance floor for movement improvisation. Then I heard Ron's singing on the CD of cellist Elizabeth Byrd called *Breath and the Chakras* and I realized Ron is also a wonderful singer. Ron embodies all the Breath, Pulse and Movement characteristics I have learned from Music for People as an expressive artist who sings, dances and drums.

I'll never forget my first experience jamming with Ron and two veteran improv artists. Catherine Marie Charlton is a recording artist, singer, dancer and improvising pianist, and Stuart Fuchs is a charismatic and remarkably gifted guitarist fluent in many styles of music.

We began the jam with Catherine starting to play this amazing music. I felt like a deer in headlights because I couldn't even move my hands to my bass. I waited quite a while before playing some long tones over Catherine's sumptuous harmonic chords. Stuart created some colorful textures with his guitar. Ron was half sleeping on the couch, and I wondered when he would get up and play. His eyes were closed and he was just taking in the moment.

As the music began to build, I watched Ron slowly open his eyes and begin to move in super-slow motion toward his collection of percussion instruments spread out on the floor. I could see he was moving in the spirit of the music, and it seemed like his body was calling him to a special instrument. He picked up a rattling gourd like a snake preparing to strike, and then rattled the shaker intensely. I had never seen anything like that before: it was as though something was brewing in his body and suddenly erupted.

Ron kept up his special blend of movements and intense percussion sounds through the length of the piece as he moved from one instrument to the next. When we hit a groove, Ron played his percussion instrument while his body reflected the sound in movement.

Boy did he bring life to that music! It was exciting, emotional and dramatic!

I got to know Ron and took advantage of every opportunity to make music with him from that day on. Ron expresses his music through his body in much the same way I later observed singer Rhiannon prepare a groove in a voice improvisation circle. The music seems to come through his body as he listens and responds to its feelings. Ron says:

Before Music for People, I was a back-up singer and support drummer in some bands, and I was getting very bored. I went to Music for People in hopes it could lead me to a more fulfilling experience. And it was just that.

I remember when I did my first three-minute improvisation solo at Omega in 1988. In those days when someone would be offering up their solo, David Darling would listen, observe and take notes on all the positive attributes of what made that improvisation work. After it was over, he would offer a critique to the group at large. It was in those comments where I absorbed all his words like a sponge. He said "Use everything that is in you and don't negate it. Let it be a positive."

I took that to heart. When I closed my eyes, I conjured whatever feelings I felt at that instant. It comes from nothing—and then there is this compulsion, nervousness and opportunity to let something come out.

Before a volcano erupts there's a great deal stirring around inside it, and when it explodes, it spews out with all this energy. This is the way the sounds and rhythms we're making have to come out. It's really a matter of listening to yourself and responding to your feelings. I don't want to feel restrained—I want to allow the spirit of those emotions and sounds to come out and I give myself full permission to do so.

Ron told me he was a singer as a child—but he was always tapping around when he heard music, so his parents bought him some drums. Now he labels himself "a melodic drummer." "I'm always singing a song to myself when I'm drumming," he says. "I hear melodies whether they are played or not—and then I drum along with them."

When I asked Ron how he became interested in dance and movement, he traced his interest to working a construction job when he was just nineteen years old. He said he used to wield a pick and shovel eight hours a day.

Swinging a pick and shovel creates a rhythm that engages your whole body. And if you really pay attention to dance movements, you are doing a lot of bending and swinging. I discovered during those long days of wielding this pick and ax that if I was angry at something, I could simply imagine I was beating the devil! And this encouraged me to let my sound and feelings come out in music and dance improvisation. People notice my movement when I am playing, and I think most of it comes from my time in that construction pit.

Ron told me that African dance and drumming both engage and unleash what he calls his playful, inner monkey—a spirit of humor and reckless, uninhibited joy. It engages his breath, voice, body movement and silliness. Starting from that early exploration of rhythm while wielding an ax, drawing on his interests as a singer and then in dance and musical improvisation, Ron has found a unique medium for his own self expression—one that uses both voice and body to the fullest.

Mindi Turin: Connecting with the Voice of Your Guitar

Mindi Turin is a singer-songwriter and another remarkable graduate from David Darling's Music for People leadership program. Her story is a reminder that all our spirit, breath, body and rhythm skills may not bring out the life in music unless they are accompanied by a degree of discipline and integrity.

Yes, it is indeed possible to access spirit and inspiration with a beginner's technique, limited facility and a lot of heart. But when artists are fluent in their craft—their instrument, voice or keyboard—the possibilities for self expression are far richer. There is a direct relationship between personal satisfaction and those hours of practice that can increase your musical facility!

When Mindi joined Music for People she was hoping the program would teach her how to play the guitar. While watching the players at Music for People she realized that the level of mastery she wanted was possible only through engaging in some kind of specialized technical study. To that point she had only played folk guitar, accompanying her voice. After her first Music for People weekend she began a formal study of guitar (including music theory) and eventually spent a week at a jazz guitar workshop at Berkeley. Still, she was frustrated at not being able to find people her own age and level of skill with a similar passion for learning. She was surrounded instead by young people who had been playing their instruments for years. Mindi says:

> My desire to play guitar was reignited during my first weekend at MfP, after which I began taking private lessons, which included theory (which I love). After about a year of casually approaching my playing, I became determined to increase my mastery, and I committed to regular lessons and practice. About four years later, I felt accomplished enough to take a summer course of one week at Berkeley. This showed me how much I didn't know and what I needed to learn. That was last year. Now I am seriously studying music at a local community college.

> I want to leap forward, but at my age, my fingers are slow, my brain is slow. I'm getting feedback from my teachers that I'm musical, especially when I'm singing. The first time I got up and sang a solo in at MfP, I improvised a bluesy thing. I'm rarely nervous about using my voice. But when I pick up my guitar I get nervous. I want to be able to sing a line and make it sing on the guitar too! It is so frustrating to me, not having this instrumental skill. On the other hand, I love playing guitar and learning about music so much that I am not deterred by my limitations. This is something I intend to do for the rest of my life, in one form or another.

Music for People is an inspiring setting. Connecting with others who loved music re-fueled my desire to become better at the guitar. The environment was always warm and accepting—but it was still a personal struggle to deal with not being picked to jam with the best improvisers. I knew I had to study between workshops in order to gain more advanced technical skills. I have to do this every week!

And the thing is—now I am willing to push through all of that, to get to something I really want—to get the prize!

You can play with all the feeling in the world, lay your heart and soul on the table with sincerity and commitment—but if you can't play in tune or communicate in a recognizable rhythmic and harmonic language you are compromising your artistry and limiting your potential. You can improve and acquire musical and technical skills at any age. So what we are striving for is a balance that includes a combination of discipline with the essential elements of Breath, Pulse and Movement—topped off with that special ingredient, you yourself!

That's the recipe here!

So as we approach the end of our exploration of how to bring music to life, remember the prerequisite for this path will likely include some long hours spent alone mastering your instrument or voice. Being able to pour your entire life experience, feeling and passion into just one note or phrase "in the moment" means having a life experience that includes those technical skills, too.

Mary Knysh: Finding Your Sound, Finding Yourself—It's *You!*

Everyone has a marvelous musician within themselves. How can I convince you of that simple fact?

Mary Knysh has been in the front of the Music for People organization, co-teaching with David Darling and inspiring countless musicians to step into the world of improvisation. It has been an honor and joy to have her as an education partner, helping me broaden my understanding of improvisation over the years. And here's the biggest lesson she has taught me: It's *you!* It's *me!*

It really doesn't matter what instrument or what kind of music you chose to play: first of all, it has to come from *you!* Our musical expression comes through *us!* And you know, it's not really ours in the first place—we don't own it. We may be the messenger, but that's only part of the story. Music is a gift, as they say. First it's a gift to us and then it's a gift we give to others. It is our responsibility to share our inspiration and pass it along. But before we pass it on we have to own it and embrace it with all its glory. It lives in our bodies for a moment and then we get to re-create it through the medium of our own unique personalities and skills.

Mary had a wealth of feelings to express with her instruments but it took the Music for People environment with its simple forms of improvisation to teach her to connect with those feelings and send them back out into the world.

I lived in the Caribbean when I was a teenager, and traveled back and forth visiting our friends that lived there from the time I was three years old. I had already been studying world music and drumming and was playing in a purely improvisational band, Heart Like A Feather, where the three of us in the band all were multi-instrumentalists exploring the merging of world music and improvisation. I played folk music on lots of instruments including the guitar, mandolin, my recorders, flutes, and percussion.

Jonathan Edwards had worked with David for several years prior to me meeting David in 1994 when we did our first recording together. By that time I was ready and eager to find more tools to take the improvisational work that I was already doing into the classroom and out into the world by means of becoming a facilitator of David's work.

With David, it was not just a matter of being present in your body via the tai chi movements, but being present in your own sound. You learned to love your own solos and stand in your own light. David had a philosophy that was so simple, it worked on every level. I took David's tools and wove them into my Orff work, which allowed me to make a connection between my instrument and myself. I felt the connection between my heartbeat and my drums. I learned to take a world groove, create my own version of it, then come back to the original groove. I learned a simple rhythm pattern (ostinato) and began to solo over it. It was so simple. I learned about myself.

Young kids could do it, too. I saw these simple techniques were empowering kids and adults to find their own music. We can all step in and take a risk, open the door, look foolish, be a learner. You don't have to know what's going to happen. Laugh at yourself. Become open and silly instead of trying to be great. That's what is so great. It's *you!!!* It's amazing, empowering and simple.

Everyone is a marvelous musician and has that capacity within them. Find your own sound—and allow yourself to be influenced by other cultures as well. David would say: I believe in you and I want to hear you and know your sound!

Both Mary and I owe David so much for what we have learned from the world of improvisation. It has freed us up to experience what it is like making music in the moment and to realize that this is where true inspiration resides.

My "In the Moment" Improvisation Experience

One of my favorite improvisation sessions took place in the fall of 2006 at a Music for People weekend course held at the Jeronomo Conference Center in Walker Valley, New York. I was jamming with three other outstanding string players and our quartet included violin, viola, cello and bass. The physical feeling of surrendering myself mind, body and soul to a palate of string textures was much like entering a dream world. When I awoke from my improvisational zone I could recall parts of the dream and the feelings I felt while playing, but I didn't remember many of the specifics.

I found myself naturally closing my eyes as I entered that state, responding to sounds, textures, energies and feelings. The amazing part was that I felt little control over what I played. It was more as though the ensemble was playing me.

When all the strings played with a single quality of sound, my fingers just found the right notes on my bass. When the energy picked up and a groove or ostinato evolved, whatever sound needed to come from my instrument managed to emerge within this texture. When there was silence, I didn't have to think about starting to play again: it either happened naturally, or I found myself responding to the other players as they entered. And playing a solo over the texture of the string ensemble was exciting and effortless—it felt like body surfing in the ocean. I got to be in the front of the wave, but I could also feel myself being carried and supported by the players around me.

Free improvisation comes from my body core, my heart and my breath. I have found myself breathing like I have never breathed before. I've played while groaning, breathing the rhythm and melodies through my mouth, whispering the melodic phrases and occasionally singing along in resonance with my inner voice. Now I understand what Glenn Gould was up to when he sang along as he played Bach with such full attention!

I especially love improvising duets with another instrument or voice—it is a true musical conversation that lives in the moment. I enjoy playing in the shadow of my partners as they play a rather slow melody, playing just a millisecond behind them on random pitches that all sound good. Duet shadowing is like being led by a wonderful dancer on the dance floor, but in this case it is a duet in sound. And believe it or not, there are *no wrong notes* in this kind of improvisation! And the *Yea energy* is when I get to let my sound and feelings completely hang out, acting silly, rambunctious, aggressive, or playful with my bass.

There are simple formats that can help organize free improvisation into a cohesive-sounding piece. For example ABA form is very common and makes a lot of musical sense. That means you begin with one idea (A). This evolves into a contrasting idea (B) and then returns to the initial idea (A). Another form, ABCA, can include a quiet opening idea of soft, non-rhythmic sounds (A) which evolve into a more exciting groove (B), then solos can begin on top of the groove (C), the piece finally returning to some kind of peaceful ending (A). And you can color the movements in your form with different feelings—stillness, movement, chaos, resolution. The only limit is your imagination.

Music is exciting when everyone is listening, allowing other members in the group to be heard, responding to and participating in the sounds that are evolving and surrendering to the overall musical direction of the ensemble. I love being both a witness and a journeyman. And when it is over I emerge from this dream-like state with an intimately personal experience with my musical colleagues. It is purely in the moment—and it is purely *me/us/ you!*

When I play classical music these days my goal is to return to this same state of mind in which every note spontaneously follows every other note as in an improvisation. The notes and rhythms may be predetermined but there are still aspects of the sound that can be improvised and still be musical.

Accelerando and *ritards* (getting faster and slower) can be played differently every day. There are places where dynamics can be reversed so that you play loud instead of soft. Feelings and expression don't have to have the same shade of color for every performance. When Mozart writes *Allegro Appassionato,* it means *exciting*—and there can be many shades of excitement that can work in the same piece of music. You can play it passionately, energetically, anxiously, desperately, suspensefully, recklessly, rambunctiously or breathlessly and still be faithful to the indication of *Allegro Appassionato.*

Your physical energy, the intensity of your emotional state and the energy of your colleagues can and will differ from day by day—and you can still allow Mozart, Schubert or Brahms to sing through you. How do *you* feel this day? It's about *you* and your state of being. It's still *you!*

I believe that studying improvisation is the quickest, purest and simplest way to enter the world of living music. Once you become comfortable with being in the musical moment it's a feeling that lives in your body and can be returned to again and again. You will meet your inner voice. You will journey into your own soul. Once you find that sweet spot you will like it—you will *love* it—and you will look for and find it in every other kind of artistic expression!

You will meet yourself.

Chapter 9
Chasing the Rainbow

I was driving across the seven-mile-long bridge that connects the peninsula south of San Francisco to the East Bay city of San Mateo one day. The San Mateo bridge was the longest bridge in the world when it was built in 1929; it is mostly a causeway with just under two miles dedicated to the high-rise section above the water—and the causeway portion allows for driving close to water level for a long section with the illusion that you are actually driving on the water. That day, an afternoon shower combined with scattered rain clouds to produce the most colorful rainbow at the water's edge.

I have never seen a rainbow frame the road so beautifully and with such symmetry. I drove my car directly into the center of this colorful crescent, going toward what seemed like a fantasy world built on an endless road. I felt I could drive right up to the rainbow's edge, seeing and feeling the vivid reality of those fast-approaching colors.

As I drove into the rainbow, of course, it seemed to be constantly moving just a little further away. And the closer I came the more the colors seemed to blend into the water and surrounding landscape. I had myself believing I was actually getting closer to where the rainbow touched the water—then realized I had been completely caught up in the illusion.

And given the chance, I'd drive deep into that rainbow again…

As musicians, poets, dancers and expressive artists of all sorts we spend our lives chasing the joyous rainbows that live within our various arts. We long to be inspired by something greater than ourselves, and the joy is in the chase—it's a healthy addiction, an endless pursuit—and it feels so good!

Our journey through *Bringing Music to Life* has been about chasing the spirit that inspires creative artists. I believe it is the same spirit that can be experienced in nature—but it permeates our bodies and resonates with others as we channel our inspiration through the creative arts.

I have been reflecting on my rainbow-like experiences in the arts, and I notice there is a common thread to them that goes straight to the core of my soul. I am speaking about those moments of excitement that take my breath away, when I can no longer contain my emotions—when my whole body trembles. I am speaking about the feelings I have when I experience something so much greater than myself that I simply surrender.

Reverend Ted Karpf, a Canon at Washington's National Cathedral wrote in praise of Don Campbell's most recent book, *Sound Spirit*:

> The sounds of faith—from Sufi chants to Hindu mantras—remind us that the music of the spheres is in our bones before it reaches our minds.

That catches something of the profundity of it. Music is my passion and it gives me wonderful opportunities to grow, to learn about myself, to learn about the world, to communicate with others—and to stay within the cycle of inspiration.

David Darling says:

When you hear the groove of many drums, you want to join in. You have a natural curiosity, you want to participate, you want to play—it's a natural human response. It is just so inviting—it's just unbelievable to be a part of that.

This natural human wish to chase after moments of beauty is the first part of a much fuller circle.

I believe we are connected to this planet and the universe through our love of nature and other human beings. When we join in this circle we can feel part of something greater than ourselves. Deepak Chopra, in the video *The Wonder of You* from the Institute of Noetic sciences, says:

The body tracks the movements of stars and planets— our biological rhythms are actually the symphony of the cosmos. There is an inner intelligence in your body, and that inner intelligence is consciousness: it is the ultimate and supreme genius which mirrors the universe.

The arts are one of the ways we can make this connection, this inner intelligence, come alive. And this may be part of the mystery as to why we have such a physical and emotional reaction to the music of our ancestors.

Imagine the grand cosmic loop. Imagine a circle of energy that begins with the vastness of space and includes that spectacular rainbow and all of nature, which pulls on us, inspiring us constantly. That's just the beginning, but it's enough for me to suggest that we need to be still and silent so we can internalize that pull, that sense of beauty and inspiration in our bodies and begin to translate this inspiration into some form of art. As we embody this life and spirit we continue the circle within our bodies. As Chunliang Al Huang suggests, we connect with the core of the earth, drawing on the energy of gravity, the inspiration of air, fire, water and earth—and even the wisdom of those who preceded us. As we gather this energy and inspiration it builds within our bodies to the point where it spills out, erupting in the form of music making, poetry, works of art, dance...until rhythm and song fill the world with our expressions of life.

And at last we are depleted, we are empty, we need to be nourished again. We return for more.

This may sound idealistic—but it is in fact the deep circle we humans have been following since the beginning of our existence: the beauty circuit, the most fulfilling circuit of all, and it continues to this day into the future.

In chapter 2 Chungliang Al Huang told us:

> Open yourself, watch it come in and fill this life as spirit, as breath. And then it comes out through our body. We keep filling up with it and emptying it out into the world as love and sound and life. It is like food for our soul, spirit and body. We are free to receive this inspiration and transform it into music, art, movement and life.

Let's take a closer look at this circle of inspiration as it breathes life into our artistic expressions. The first part includes the seductive power of beauty—my rainbow, the music you love—which attracts and inspires us to translate it into some form of expression. What kind of music motivates you? What kind of rainbow do you want to follow? For some the beauty manifests in musical discipline and perfection; for others it lives in harmony or rhythm. Perhaps you are fascinated with the repetitive power of chant, ragas, or sacred dances.

Don Campbell says:

From the chants of each society and religion, we can learn how these groups heal, soothe and save. From their dances, we can learn how they move, love and fight. Even the most radical cheerleaders of gospel music or African drumming call down the Holy Spirit to cast out evil. By tone, melody, text or drumbeat, auditory stimuli organize the brain and body for an experience through which we connect with the unseen. This is the breath of life, the impetus to grow.

Lynn Miller is a gifted expressive arts therapist who directs voice improvisations in the Music for People program. She describes how inspiration travels through her body and voice and becomes for her a spiritual connection:

What really excites me is the flow—it is effortless, it is magical, and it creates a spiritual connection. Whether I am facilitating, coaching or singing, it goes beyond myself. What comes out is often more beautiful than anything I could have thought up—even though I am the one who "did" it. It's like living in a dream. This is the magical place where I'm inspired to be, and where I want to return.

It's something to do with opening my heart. It's about really listening for guidance without thinking about it. I feel this great connection to nature, to the earth, to the universe and to our creator. It just keeps on going. It's infinite. This is my goal. And the voice is my easiest entrance, because it is so connected to the body. Breath gives you both an inner and an outer experience.

We have been taught by our culture that we have to keep our own mind, body and feelings separate from the world—but when through our art we have this experience of reunion, we remember—Oh yes! We are all one, we are all connected with the universe and with each other. We are always joining together so we can be part of something greater. We are all part of the source.

Unison is the truth, harmony is where we are going.

In Asian cultures, *yin* and *yang* provide contrast, balance and completeness. In the arts, I would compare the *yang* to the high, outgoing energy of a spiritually triumphant Mahler symphony or the show-stopping finale from the musical *New York, New York*—and I'd contrast it with the introverted, soulful spirit of the Irish ballad *Danny Boy* or the slow movement of a Mozart piano sonata. All have their place in the arts, and there's probably a touch of quiet introversion in the most extrovert of pieces, a touch of movement in the quietest and most lyrical.

Let's be clear on this: in the words of Ecclesiastes, "To every thing there is a season." There is a place for virtuosity, adrenaline, discipline, fire, strength and power. These qualities in music, as in life, are something to marvel at and appreciate—both tantalizing and inspiring. Yet while I love this very positive *Yea* energy, I am also drawn to music that speaks specifically and generously to my soul and to my sense of being home. It goes far deeper. This is a spirit that I have described in nature, but in my art it takes the form of humbling, heartfelt and indelibly memorable music.

I believe that acknowledging the magic that speaks directly to my soul validates my own pursuit of the rainbow, of the vitality and spirit of beauty as my primary goal in being an artist. This is what is most real for me. As I now share some of these personal experiences, I hope to remind you once again of what makes your own pursuit of beauty in the arts so enriching and life-giving.

I remember 9/11.

When I recall my most profound musical experiences I return first to that fateful day in 2001 when the world was brought to a halt in disbelief that such tragedy could strike New York City, Washington DC and Pennsylvania. What I remember from that horrific week was Denyce Graves singing *America the Beautiful* and *The Lord's Prayer* during the memorial service honoring the victims of 9/11 at the Washington National Cathedral. Her performance evoked tears of grief at the time and feelings in me that are still as vivid as if it were yesterday. Her singing remains part of my body and soul.

When our art connects us to such an historical event, to the death of a loved one or to some large or impressive events in life or nature, we feel touched by something much greater than ourselves. But not everything is on this grand scale. Life's small discoveries can be enchanting, too.

I'd like to fast-forward, then, to everyday life and the pursuit of artistic pleasures that aren't necessarily connected to profound events or earthshaking moments. Performing arts can provide a wonderful escape from our busy, bustling, monetary, industrial and technological society. Spending a few hours in the week attending a concert, play or movie can bring comfort, peace, joy and rejuvenation to mind, body and spirit. The arts are food for the soul. They not only nourish us but have the power to heal and inspire us, too.

I recall one very short moment in sound that took my breath away. It may only have lasted a matter of seconds, but the experience was so vivid that it leaps to mind when I think of these things. It was the fall of 2007 and I was at a San Francisco Symphony performance conducted by Michael Tilson Thomas with flute soloist Paula Robison performing Thomas's *Notturno* for flute and orchestra.

Tilson Thomas describes it as a "a virtuoso piece evoking the lyrical world of Italian music," but it wasn't the virtuoso brilliance that was remarkable to me. The moment that really impressed me came at the very end of the piece with the very last note that Paula Robison played.

Imagine that you could pour your entire life experience into performing *just one note* perfectly. That was the kind of artistry I witnessed that night: it was Paula playing just that one, long, beautiful note. There was something magical in how she played that note which made it stand out with shimmering beauty. That one note left the audience in a state of bliss that I am sure will never be forgotten. It seemed to last forever. It took everyone's breath away.

Folk songs have a unique appeal to our souls.

They seem to tap into our deepest wellsprings of culture and pull uncontrollably on our heartstrings. When I play the opening measures of *Danny Boy* on my bass it goes right to my soul. In much the same way, I get a lump in my throat when I hear my bass colleague Diana Gannett play *Simple Gifts* and *Amazing Grace*, or Anthony Stoops' inspired arrangement of *Fantasy on Red River Valley*. Similarly, my bass buddy David Murray pulls my heartstrings with Jay Ungar's *Ashokan Farewell*. Perhaps the magic of the folk song is the connection it holds to our home, land, culture and the very earth itself, resonating deep within our bodies.

Confession time: I have to admit, too, that I love watching the TV reality shows *American Idol*, *Dancing with the Stars* and *So You Think You Can Dance*. I tell my friends I have a professional excuse for watching these shows because I'm writing this book about voice and movement, but what really interests me is watching the growth of these competing artists over the length of the series. And there are often some amazing performances. The highlight of the last two years of reality TV shows for me was a performance by two dancers in ABC's *So You Think You Can Dance*. It brought tears to my eyes.

Mia Michaels is one of the world's great contemporary choreographers. She designed a piece to the music of Billy Porter's *Time* for two gifted dancers, Niel Haskell and Lacey Schwimmer. The piece is about Mia reuniting in heaven with her deceased father for one final dance. Michaels' choreography, Porter's music, the costumes, sets and the performance of these two dancers all came together in such a perfect integration of forces, coupled with the heartfelt storyline that it brought all these elements to life. And once again (as we saw in chapter 7) it wasn't just one thing that did the trick—it was the complete package. That dance went right to the heart, and it still lives in my body as if it was my own personal experience.

Touching the Soul Goes Very Deep

Julie Weber directs the music leadership program at Music for People and is a creative composer, pianist, singer, educator and master improviser herself. She moderates the two-disc CD set *Conversations with David Darling* that explores the many principles of improvisation taught at Music for People and has a gift for articulating the feelings that are evoked by listening to music.

Julie talks about the power of the circle that I spoke of earlier in a way that helps me understand my own listening experience. When music finds its origins in spirit, incarnates in the form of a contemporary performer and then communicates itself to the listener, there's a sense of completion, of coming full circle. This loop, as Julie calls it, is the embodiment of the powerful inspiration present when music becomes a living thing.

Julie describes the experience of listening to the great cellist Mstislav Rostropovich:

There are times when I hear a particular piece of music or a certain performer, and I am drawn into the music, rapt with attention and deep emotion, because I know I am in the presence of something extraordinary.

These occasions create such an imprint in me that they become unforgettable, visceral memories, that I can recall just by remembering the feelings I had at that moment. There is an innate understanding that I am in the realm of the profound, that this is a reflection of the great mystery and wonder, beyond our earth world and human lives.

I listened to a collection of cello performances by the famed Mstislav Rostropovich recently. And okay, it's a given that his skill is top level, and that alone obviously offers a kind of excitement. But I was blown away by the *quality* of the sound, a quality that immediately, in just a few notes, moved me into another dimension. When I am moved this way, I really mean physically as well as emotionally or intellectually, I get a tug at my sternum that feels like I am being lifted up towards the experience. I felt respect, involvement, reverence, curiosity, interest, absorption, incomprehension, fascination, enlightenment, excitement, stimulation, engagement, enthrallment, immersion, all welling up inside me, invoked by those sounds... I could go on.

And this was on a car stereo.

It really put the question to me: What is this all about? I couldn't stop listening. It seems to me that Rostropovich was so at one with his instrument and with the music he played, that he could communicate the heart of the music beyond the notes on the page, to produce a sound that in some mysterious way utterly transcends time and space. It goes beyond being an inspirational listening experience... somewhere else.

I have been opened in various ways to areas of experience and expression that go deeper, that go beyond the notes and rhythms, beyond my innate love and appreciation of the intricacies and splendors of music, into a place with more dimension, more insight, more connection.

What is it that makes this so memorable, even awesome? What awakens us to the understanding that we are in the presence of greatness? It's a question I keep asking myself each time I have such an experience. And I have concluded that although many elements in music making can be exciting, the *life* in music must form what I call a loop.

It is not the performer alone who creates this experience for the listener. It is not a person, ensemble, instrument or sound, it's not talent or genius alone that gives us this experience. Even the performer, if he or she is to experience such life force while playing, must be involved in a bigger loop that goes far beyond technical skills and instrument. There has to be a convergence of cooperation between the source, the individual or group, and the time and place—an energetic communion. We must be attuned—tuned in to the station, so to speak—and have a certain readiness and willingness and offer a particular kind of attention, to allow the magic to manifest.

So then there's a further loop: from receptivity, via engagement, to reaction, then interaction.

I believe Julie is talking about being tuned in to the true source of magic—the life in music. When we directly connect with the greater energy we feel it as if we are a part of it. We have made contact with inspiration from the source and transcended time, sound, performer and medium. This is the life. This is the spirit. And we are inseparably connected to it.

The Nature of Life and Spirit on Earth

The original meaning of spirit, from the Latin *spiritus*, is to blow, to breathe, and many languages use the same word for the concepts of *spirit*, *breath* and *wind*. Don Campbell, in his book *Sound Spirit*, reminds us:

Spirit is greater than an individual: it's tangible whether seen or unseen, heard or unheard. It's commonly referred to as "the source out of which all things are created." Spirit brings us to a state of wonder. From ancient chants to folk songs and dance, the power of music instantly connects us with the past, present and future.

We can be inspired by mystics and musicians through listening. We can dance with the African shamans, the Haitian Christians and Native Americans. Music can transport us to a better place. *Vibration* is the center of all life. We are most alive when we sing together. Your spirit is alive, so let it dance and rejoice.

This is the breath of life, the impetus to grow. Our body, emotions and minds may not always be in harmony, but together they create the drive to express and communicate. Sound and rhythm set the foundation of our understanding of the world around us.

In *The Mastery of Music*, Joshua Bell spoke about being nervous before his first entrance as the soloist in the Beethoven *Violin Concerto* because he has to wait several minutes for the orchestra introduction before he plays his first note. But then he experiences a sense of calm just as he is about to play:

It is as though I must succumb to this world that Beethoven has created, and I suppose I almost treat it in a religious sort of way. I feel as though I surrender to this. I feel that there is somebody who knows this world so much better than I do—and it is Beethoven himself, who created it—and there is something very comforting about that.

This is where words fail us.

Is Joshua Bell tapping into the cosmic spirit of Beethoven, as though his great predecessor was leaning over his shoulder, whispering to him, and turning the pages for him—or is his exquisite knowledge of the great master's music and innate sympathy for it at work—or both?

Are they even perhaps the same thing?

Great musicians remind us that there is both an intuitive component to the inspiration the great composers bring us and that they leave in their scores and writings some pretty straightforward earthy guidance.

In one sense, then, when we play their music we are transcending time and reincarnating the beauty and inspiration they glimpsed into today's world. In bringing these great moments to life a performing artist's success is inseparably tied to the ability to dig deep within the soul and express the special energy found there. How do we channel this age-old inspiration in our contemporary bodies? Charles Cameron offers us his insights on making these connections as he describes the power of silence as the bridge to this inspiration.

Following the Silence

There is a deep well of silence within,
all music begins from it,
ringing faintly in our ears
at first, then building,
bursting from listening
into sound, into making music,
the whole body rocks,
the arms lift, throat opens, voice spills

upon the wide air,
slips into the listening ear,
sounds and resounds in heart's
four chambers,
touches the well of silence within:
silence at music's birth, at music's end

Charles Cameron
Written for Barry Green

Silence is our way in.

There is an exercise everyone does before they begin each musical improvisation at David Darling's improvisation workshops. It begins with inhaling and raising your hands above your head. Then as you exhale, you drop your hands and…wait. This brings us to a moment of silence which David suggests should precede the beginning of all improvisations. He says:

> Everything has to do with the breath. There is nothing difficult about participating, because we all breathe. We inhale and we exhale, and it is so simple to just join in. You don't have to think about it. Just take a breath, pause…and start.

> When you hear the first sound, if you are listening, it will become your teacher.

David says that the exhale is our magic. When we are sitting quietly and attentively before a performance we are connected with the universe, and the music that results is much deeper and has so much more feeling. If you take the time to connect with silence before you play it becomes very simple: you are able to let go of your agendas and enter a very calm place, a place that is peaceful and void of ego. You enter the world of spontaneity and your music is fresh.

This breathing and silence exercise still requires discipline, because the nagging, grown-up voice in your head will likely want to push its way in past the silence and tell you what to do, when to play and in general, take over your improvisation. If you really listen to the silence that follows your breath and wait, you can tame the mind and play from a profoundly natural place.

David feels the intuition and knowledge that resides in silence is part of a universal wisdom that can guide our performance. He talks about the beginning of an improvisation when four people are sitting in silence, not worrying about when or what to play. They just wait together with trust that something will happen and see what emerges.

> As we sit in silence, we are listening to the sound of the universe. At the moment we are called to action—to poetry, speech, song or rhythm—we are already in a profound relationship with life.

> It is a matter of welcoming that exciting moment, a moment of human dialogue with nature and with the universe. We are never soloists, you know, silence is our duet partner— we are always playing a duet with silence.

> Musicians should really give thanks to *silence*—it is our way in.

> When you meet people who practice yoga or mediation or any other age-old discipline of that sort, they will tell you that *silence* is one of the great avenues which brings people to the place of balance in life, which brings both joy and pragmatism. You cannot have joy without silence.

> And your personal silence before you play is when you see the fundamentals of life.

Ekhart Tolle, the German spiritual teacher and author of the best seller *The Power of Now*, tells us that when you lose touch with your inner stillness you lose touch with yourself. When you lose touch with yourself you lose yourself in the world. Your innermost sense of who you are is inseparable from stillness.

I have learned so much from taking time to connect with silence before I play. Silence comes *before* you even connect with your music. If you are improvising, then your improvisation should come out of nowhere. And even if you are playing written music, you will benefit from connecting with silence before you bring on the spirits of Beethoven or Ellington.

> Silence is like a lake,
> music like the reflections in that lake:
> music wouldn't be there
> without silence,
> silence gathers itself into sound
> if you wait for it,
> silence ripples into sound,
> silence cascades into sound,
>
> you can cup silence in your hands
> and drink it,
> if you listen to silence
> the sea will be in your ears—
> cupping your hands for silence
> you may fetch music for others to drink.

Charles Cameron
Written for Barry Green

Feeding the Soul Is Growing

The pull of the rainbow, the beauty of the sunset, a giant grove of tall redwoods, the vast endless horizon seen across ocean waters, majestic waterfalls, great mountains and rivers—all remind us of our humble human existence on this grand planet Earth.

I believe that when we resonate with nature, when we resonate with other artists—both those in our own lives and those who have come before us—we affirm our existence through our songs and movements.

How can we sustain and nurture the soul? What does this mean, what form does it take? How do we keep the spirit alive? What gives us the inspiration to stay on this path?

Honesty, sincerity, commitment and humility are good pathways. I feel it is very important to follow our own rainbows, our own glimpses of the beautiful, the profound, the true. When we do this we are reminded that we need not do it alone. We can sustain our journey with inspiration and guidance from others and from within.

This path will be different for each individual. It is *you* and only *you* who can set out on *your* path. There is a deep and unique relationship between your inner voice and the life force within your artistic expression. When you nurture your body you are feeding your soul. This is how you can grow as an individual and in community with others.

In his book *Having it All*, Phil Porter writes that we *are* our bodies.

All of our experience is physical. Feelings are physical. Inspiration is a physical experience. You know when you are in love by feeling. Spirit is ultimately experiential, not philosophical. We would not be able to recognize a spiritual experience unless there was something going on in our bodies. Spirit should not be exclusively wrapped in and around theology and religion. Spirit issues are body issues, mind issues and heart issues. If we see them as integrated into our lives, rather than being set apart, we will more likely to experience wholeness.

The Final Step: Follow Your Rainbow!

François Rabbath is my bass teacher. He is my bass guru! I will never play the bass as he does. No one can—and no one should even try. But François has inspired me to learn how I can be a better bass player, to understand the instrument in a new way and to use it to communicate what inspires me as a musician. François' spirit transcends his playing, and that's why I want to follow the rainbow that radiates in him and is also present in me. He has taught me that the bass is the voice of my soul and that I can share this with others through my own interpretation of music. Then I can let my own rainbow shine.

I have been inspired to learn about music in ways that go far beyond being a bass player from several mentors. I am thinking here of W. Timothy Gallwey, with whom I set out on this journey so many years ago, of W. A. Mathieu, Don Campbell, and my loving wife and spiritual muse, the Reverend Mary Tarbell-Green—and especially of the composer, cellist, and master improviser, David Darling, whose personal mentoring, generous soul and brilliant methodology for teaching have made him my greatest inspiration in writing *Bringing Music to Life*.

Like my attempt to chase down the rainbow on that bridge across the Bay, this work represents a journey and not its ending. These are my teachers. It is their inspiration that makes me want to stay on this road. They have helped me learn about myself and about the world all around and even ahead of me. We are all students. We are never too old to study. My teachers have teachers, too.

And I think this is a significant point to make as we come to the end of our journey together. The greatest musicians on this planet are also the greatest students. They never stop learning, they are constantly reinventing themselves. It is an honor to follow in their footsteps.

We began *Bringing Music to Life* by noticing that the life and spirit in music comes into you and through your body and passes out into the world. It comes through you alive, *pulsating* in time, through your transformed *breath,* and through every cell of your *body.* And the magic comes with a natural integration of these three elements with the unconscious surrender to the spirit.

You have only one body and, perhaps only one life on Earth. Take care of it. Feed it. Nurture it. Enjoy it. Allow yourself to be a student of the pulse. Study and develop your voice. Buy a drum, tap along with others and improvise. Notice the rhythm of life in your walking and talking. Notice the rhythms in nature and music. Listen to music from all around the world. Learn about ragas, try out some of the eastern movement disciplines and study all kinds of dance.

And become a student of your inner silence. Love the silence. Embrace the silence. Listen to the silence—and follow its direction.

Then jam, scat, move and groove!

Chase the rainbow—follow your dreams. Bring it to life!

Acknowledgments
Barry Says, "Thank You"

Thank you to my community of family, friends, colleagues, teachers and students who have make it possible for me to follow my rainbow.

To my wife, the Reverend Mary Tarbell-Green for her inspiration, resources, patience and love. To my parents Leona and Joel Green for their confidence, support and love. To my sons Zachary and Adam and their families for their tolerance. To my stepchildren Rich and Amber, my brother, cousins, aunts and uncles, nieces, nephews and grandchildren who all make me proud to be a Green!

To my mentor David Darling and the Music for People community for inspiring this work and allowing me to access what makes my music come to life: Mary Knysh, Ron Kravitz, Julie Weber, Lynn and Eric Miller, Liz Byrd, Julie Theriault, Josee Allard, Clint Goss, Lucy Michaelson, Henrik Stubbe, Holly Foster, the Oshinsky Family, Katherine Weider, Ned Leavitt, Catherine Marie Charlton, Mindi Turin, Stuart Fuchs, Heather Keller, Jane Buttars and all my improvisation colleagues.

To my Bay Area teaching colleagues who have helped me develop these concepts in the public schools and at the Golden Gate Bass Camp: movement guru Alan Scofield from Young Imaginations, jazz bassist/singer colleague Kristin Korb, rhythmic specialist Curt Moore and to the San Franscisco Symphony

Education Department: Ron Gallman, Sammi Madison, Kay Hamilton, Anastasia Herold. To public school teaching colleagues Michelle Winter, Jerry Panone, and Harvey Benstein. And thanks to my Tuesday night jammers for forcing me to take jazz solos!

My personal mentors, advisors and most artistically inspirational colleagues are David Darling, Allaudin Mathieu, Don Campbell, and François Rabbath.

Thank you to Ed and Alec Harris at GIA as well as Gregg Sewell for his copy editing and Martha Chlipala for her creative artistry on the cover for *Bringing Music to Life*. Robert Sacha designed and laid out these pages to be both elegant and readable. GIA has supported my creativity and musical projects for over thirty years! Thank you to Sharon Turney for designing the graphic used on chapter title pages.

I wish to thank John Kennedy and Owen Linderholm for helping me in proofreading the manuscript.

Special gratitude to my private editor Charles Cameron who has added a little Mozart melody to my thumpy double-bass words for *The Inner Game of Music*, *The Mastery of Music* and now *Bringing Music to Life*.

I wrote this book to help me be a better musician and a better teacher to my many young bass students. This book is really for the kids.

Resources

This modest list is included to inspire further research and inspiration in bringing music to life. Each resource may lead you to further resources. May your own journey continue beyond these initial pathways.

Books

On Improvisation

Agrell, Jeffrey. *Improvisation Games for Classical Musicians.* Chicago: GIA Publications, Inc., 2008.

Azzara, Christopher D. and Richard F. Grunow. *Developing Musicianship through Improvisation.* Chicago: GIA Publications, Inc., 2006.

Bailey. Derek. *Improvisation: Its Nature and Practice in Music.* Cambridge, MA: Da Capo Press, 1993.

Borgo, David. *Sync or Swarm: Improvising Music In A Complex Age.* New York: The Continuum International Publishing Group, 2005.

Cahn, William L. *Creative Music Making.* New York: Routledge Taylor & Francis Group, 2005.

Chase, Mildred Portney. *Improvisation: Music from the Inside Out.* Berkeley, CA: Creative Arts Book Company, 1998.

Frank, Dave with John Amaral. *Joy of Improv, Book One: Beginning the Foundation.* Milwaukee, WI: Hal Leonard Corporation, 1998.

_____. *Joy of Improv, Book Two: Completing the Foundation.*
Milwaukee, WI: Hal Leonard Corporation, 1998.

Kahle, Laura. *Music Improvisation.* Fundamentals of Music
Series Part 4. Varsity Lakes, Australia: Knowledge Books and
Software Publishing, 2005.

Kanack, Alice Kay. *Fun Improvisation for...[Violin, Viola, Cello,
and Piano].* Creative Ability Development Series. Van Nuys,
CA: Alfred Publishing, 1997.

Kanack, Alice Kay. *Musical Improvisation for Children.*
Creative Ability Development Series. Van Nuys, CA: Alfred
Publishing, 1998.

Knysh, Mary and Betsy Bevan. *A Facilitator's Guide to Boom
Do Pa: EthnicInfluenced Music Improvisation.* Millville, PA:
Rhythmic Connections.

Nachmanovitch, Stephen. *Free Play: Improvisation in Life and
Art.* New York: Tarcher/Putnam, 1990.

Oshinsky, Jim. *Return to Child: Music for People's Guide to
Improvising Music and Authentic Group Leadership.* Goshen,
CT: Music for People, 2008.

Perry, Geoffrey Fitzhugh. *Fiddle Jam: A WayCool Easy Way
to Learn How to Improvise.* Milwaukee, WI: Hal Leonard
Corporation, 2005.

Reeves, Scott D. *Creative Jazz Improvisation.* Upper Saddle
River, NJ: Prentice Hall, Inc., 1988.

Roth, Gabrielle and John Loudon. *Maps to Ecstasy: The Healing
Power of Movement.* Novato, CA: New World Library, 1998.

Rothenberg, David. *Sudden Music: Improvisation, Sound, Nature.*
Athens, GA: University of Georgia Press, 2001.

On Music

Ababio-Clottey, Aeeshah and Kokomon Clottey. *Beyond Fear: Twelve Spiritual Keys to Racial Healing.* Tiburon, CA: H J Kramer Inc, 1998.

Adolphe, Bruce. *What to Listen for in the World.* Milwaukee: Limelight Editions, 2004.

Berger, Dorita S. *Toward the Zen of Performance: Music Improvisation Therapy for the Development of Self-Confidence in the Performer.* St. Louis: MMB Music, 1999.

Bruser, Madeline. *The Art of Practicing: A Guide to Making Music from the Heart.* New York: Harmony/Bell Tower, 1999.

Campbell, Don G. *Introduction to the Musical Brain.* St. Louis: MMB Music, 1983.

_____. *The Mozart Effect: Tapping the Power of Music to Heal the Body, Strengthen the Mind, and Unlock the Creative Spirit.* New York: HarperPaperbacks, 2001.

_____. *The Mozart Effect for Children: Awakening Your Child's Mind, Health, and Creativity with Music.* New York: HarperPaperbacks, 2002.

_____. *The Roar of Silence: Healing Powers of Breath, Tone & Music.* Wheaton, IL: Quest Books, 1989.

_____. *Sound Spirit: How Our Faith Makes Us Human,* with CD. Carlsbad, CA: Hay House, 2008.

Clottey, Kokomon. *Mindful Drumming: Ancient Wisdom for Unleashing the Human Spirit and Building Community.* Oakland, CA: Sankofa Publishing, 2003.

Green, Barry. *The Inner Game of Music Workbook.* Eds. for individuals (C Instrument, B-flat, E-flat and F Instruments, Piano, and Voice) and for Small Ensembles, Band, and Orchestra. Chicago: GIA Publications, Inc., 1996.

_____. *The Mastery of Music: Ten Pathways to True Artistry.* New
York: Broadway Books, 2005.

_____ and W. Timothy Gallwey. *The Inner Game of Music.* New
York: The Doubleday Publishing Group, 1986.

_____ with Greg Lyne and Larry Ajer. *The Inner Game of Music
Workbook for Men's & Women's Barbershop Quartets,
Choruses and Classrooms.* Nashville: Barbershop Harmony
Society.

Hart, Mickey, Frederic Lieberman, and Fredric Lieberman. *Spirit
into Sound: The Magic of Music.* Petaluma, CA: Acid Test
Productions, 2006.

Hart, Mickey, Fredric Lieberman, and D. A. Sonneborn. *Planet
Drum: A Celebration of Percussion and Rhythm.* Petaluma,
CA: Acid Test Productions, 1998.

Jordan, James. *The Musician's Soul.* Chicago: GIA Publications,
Inc., 1999.

_____. *The Musician's Spirit.* Chicago: GIA Publications, Inc.,
2002.

_____. *The Musician's Walk.* Chicago: GIA Publications, Inc.,
2006.

Lauridsen, Morten, Paul Salamunovich, and James Jordan.
Dialogues, Volume 1. Chicago: GIA Publications, Inc., 2008.

Lautzenheiser, Tim. *The Art of Successful Teaching.* Chicago:
GIA Publications, Inc., 1992.

Lautzenheiser, Tim. *The Joy of Inspired Teaching.* Chicago: GIA
Publications, Inc., 1993.

_____. *Leadership: Vision, Commitment, Action.* Chicago: GIA
Publications, Inc., 2006.

Lieberman, Julie Lyonn. *Planet Musician: The World Music
Sourcebook for Musicians.* Milwaukee, WI: Hal Leonard
Corporation, 1998.

Mathieu, W. A. *The Listening Book: Discovering Your Own Music*. Boston: Shambhala Publications, 1991.

———. *The Musical Life: Reflections on What It Is and How to Live It*. Boston: Shambhala Publications, 1991.

Merritt, Stephanie. *Mind, Music & Imagery: Unlocking the Treasures of Your Mind*. Fairfield, CT: Aslan Publishing, 1996.

Noble, Weston, Charles Bruffy, and James Jordan. *Dialogues, Volume 2*. Chicago: GIA Publications, Inc., 2008.

Oshinsky, Jim. *Return to Child: Music for People's Guide to Improvising Music and Authentic Group Leadership*. Goshen, CT: Music for People, 2008.

Porter, Phil. *Having It All: Body, Mind, Heart & Spirit Together Again at Last*. Oakland, CA: Wing It! Press, 1997.

Ristad, Eloise. *The Soprano on Her Head: Right-Side-Up Reflections on Life and Other Performances*. Boulder, CO: Real People Press, 1981.

Rosas, Debbie and Carlos Rosas. *The Nia Technique: The High-Powered Energizing Workout that Gives You a New Body and a New Life*. New York: Broadway Books, 2005.

Sacks, Oliver. *Musicophilia: Tales of Music and the Brain*. New York: Knopf Publishing Group, 2007.

Stoloff, Bob. *Scat! Vocal Improvisation Techniques*. New York: Gerard and Sarzin Publishing Co., 1996.

Werner, Kenny. *Effortless Mastery: Liberating the Master Musician Within,* with DVD. New Albany, IN: Jamey Abersold Jazz, 2007.

Wis, Ramona M. *The Conductor as Leader.* Chicago: GIA Publications, Inc., 2007.

Wooten, Victor L. *The Music Lesson: A Spiritual Search for Growth Through Music*. New York: Berkeley Books, 2008.

Zander, Rosamund Stone and Benjamin Zander. *The Art of Possibility: Transforming Professional and Personal Life.* Boston: Harvard Business School Publishing, 2000.

Compact Discs

Darling, David and Julie Weber. *The Darling Conversations, Volume 1,* three-disc set. Westport, CT: Manifest Spirit Music.

Gabriel, Peter and Amanda Jones. *Voices of the Real World.* Real World/CEMA, 2000.

Mathieu, W. A. *W. A. Mathieu Reads from* The Listening Book *and* The Musical Life. Second Spirit Music, 2008.

Instructional DVDs

Aebersold, Jamey. *Jazz: Anyone Can Improvise.* New Albany, IN: Jamey Abersold Jazz, 2007.

Abramson, Robert. *Dalcroze Eurhythmics,* written and produced by Timothy Caldwell. Chicago, IL: GIA Publications, 2007.

Bach, J. S. and Bedrich Smetana. *Great Conductors in Rehearsal and Performance,* Toronto Symphony Orchestra conducted by Karel Ancerl and the CBC Toronto Chamber Orchestra conducted by Hermann Scherchen. Toronto, ON: CBC Toronto, 2005.

Beethoven, Ludwig van, Johannes Brahms, Anton Bruckner, Cesar Franck, Darius Milhaud, and Wolfgang Amadeus Mozart. *Leonard Bernstein Anniversary Box,* five-disc set, various orchestras conducted by Leonard Bernstein. Franklin, TN: Naxos of America, Inc., 2008.

_____, Alberto Ginastera, and Jose Pablo Moncayo. *The Promise of Music,* the Simón Bolívar Youth Orchestra of Venezuela, conducted by Gustavo Dudamel. Hamburg, Germany: Deutsche Grammophon, 2008.

Bernstein, Leonard. *Leonard Bernstein: The Gift of Music: An Intimate Portrait,* directed by Horant H. Hohlfeld. Hamburg, Germany: Deutsche Grammophon, 2007.

Boulez, Pierre, Christoph von Dohnányi, John Eliot Gardiner, Valery Gergiev, and Esa-Pekka Salonen. *Great Conductors in Rehearsal,* five-disc set, Esa-Pekka Salonen with the Los Angeles Philharmonic, John Eliot Gardiner and the English Baroque Soloists and Monteveredi Choir, Valery Gergiev with the Rotterdam Philharmonic Orchestra, Pierre Boulez with the Vienna Philharmonic Orchestra, and Christoph Von Dohnanyi and The Philharmonia Orchestra. Image Entertainment, 2005.

Darling, David. *Improvisation: Magical Music.* Carlisle, PA: Spahr Productions.

Dudamel, Gustavo. *60 Minutes: Gustavo the Great.* New York, NY: CBS, 2008.

Evans, Bill. *The Universal Mind of Bill Evans: Jazz Pianist on the Creative Process and Self-teaching.* New York, NY: Rhapsody Films, 2005.

Flanagan, Bob. *Bob Flanagan: Musical Improvisation.* System Yellow, 1986.

Frank, Dave. *Breakthrough to Improv: The Secrets of Improvisation: 15 Steps to Musical Freedom for All Musicians.* Milwaukee, WI: Hal Leonard Corporation, 2001.

Gabriel, Arnald D. with Tim Lautzenheiser. *Master Conductors: From the Battlefield to the Podium.* Chicago, IL: GIA Publications, 2007.

Glennie, Evelyn, Fred Frith, and Jason the Fogmaster. *Touch the Sound: A Sound Journey with Evelyn Glennie,* directed by Thomas Riedelsheimer. New Video Group, 2006.

Gould, Glenn. *Glenn Gould: The Alchemist.* EMI Classics, 2003.

_____. *The Goldberg Variations: From Glenn Gould Plays Bach,* directed by Bruno Monsaingeon. Sony Classics, 2007.

_____. *Glenn Gould: Hearafter,* directed by Bruno Monsaingeon. Juxtapositions, 2006.

Green, Barry. *Bringing Music to Life.* Chicago, IL: GIA Publications, 2009.

_____. *The Inner Game of Music.* Madison, WI: The University of Wisconsin–Madison.

Jordon, James and Eugene Migliaro Corporon. *The Anatomy of Conducting: Architecture & Essentials.* Chicago, IL: GIA Publications, 2008.

Liebman, David. *Understanding Jazz Rhythm: The Concept of Swing.* Stroudsburg, PA: Caris Music Services.

McMurray, Allan. *Conducting from the Inside Out, Disc One: Gesture and Movement,* DVD-613. Chicago, IL: GIA Publications, 2007.

_____. *Conducting from the Inside Out, Disc Two: Conductor and Composer,* DVD-697. Chicago, IL: GIA Publications, 2004.

_____. *Conducting from the Inside Out, Disc Three: Kindred Spirits,* DVD-665. Chicago, IL: GIA Publications, 2006.

Moore, Curt. *Afro-Cuban Drumset: Grooves You can Use,* directed by Larry Hauser. Lakeridge Productions, 2007.

Peterson, Oscar, Dizzy Gillespie, Norman Granz, Ray Brown, and Herb Ellis. *Oscar Peterson: Music in the Key of Oscar.* View, Inc., 2004.

Olatunji, Babatunde. *African Drumming.* Miami, FL: DCI Music Video, Inc., 1996.

Rhiannon. *Flight: Rhiannon's Interactive Guide to Vocal Improvisation: Taking Flight/Soaring.* Louisville, CO: Sounds True, Inc., 2000.

Velez, Glen. *Handdance.* CD, Nomad, 1984, 1999.

Wallace, Robert. *Learn Caxixi with Robert Wallace, the Drum Guy.* Oakland, CA: Total Rhythm.

_____. *Learn to Play Pandeiro, Volumes 1 and 2,* each volume available separately. Oakland, CA: Total Rhythm.

Websites

Note: Descriptive paragraphs are taken from the websites listed.
American Orff-Schulwerk Association

http://aosa.org/

> *The American Orff-Schulwerk Association is a professional organization dedicated to the creative teaching approach developed by Carl Orff and Gunild Keetman. We are united by our belief that music and movement—to speak, sing and play; to listen and understand; to move and create—should be an active and joyful experience.*

attacca percussion group • Adam Green

http://attaccapercussiongroup.com/

> *A unique ensemble that brings a fresh attitude to chamber music.*

The Attitudinal Healing Connection of Oakland • Kokomon Clottey

http://ahc-oakland.org/

> *Attitudinal Healing is a non-traditional mental health program based on the belief that the purpose of all communication is for joining and not separation. It is the process of learning to let go of painful, fearful attitudes about our life experiences and learning to choose love not fear, peace not conflict, and how we can forgive others so that we can forgive ourselves.*

Beverly Botsford
> http://ibiblio.org/musicians/beverly_botsford.html
>> *Cross-cultural percussionist, educator, movement specialist, and drum maker.*

Jane Buttars
> http://cdbaby.com/cd/buttars
>> *Keys to the Inside is strikingly original, intensely expressive, beautifully crafted music by an exceptional artist. Live solo piano improvisations on the creative edge.*

Cold Mountain Music • W. A. Mathieu
> http://coldmountainmusic.com/
>> *The Music and Writing of William Allaudin Mathieu.*

Dalcroze Society of America
> http://dalcrozeusa.org/
>> *The Dalcroze approach to music learning teaches musical concepts through rhythmic movement, expressive aural training, and physical, vocal, and instrumental improvisation.*

Dancing Hands Music
> http://dancinghands.com/
>> *Instructional materials related to drumming and rhythm.*

Drum Café • Arthur Hull
> http://drumcircles.com/
>> *Team building and interactive drumming entertainment and leadership programs.*

Drum Circle Music • Kalani
> http://drumcirclemusic.com/
>> *An approach to facilitating drum circles, rhythm-based events, music, movement, voice, body percussion and other forms of creative arts in a group setting.*

Eric Edberg
http://ericedberg.wordpress.com/
> *Blog of professional cellist and professor of music at DePauw University School of Music. Features an extensive list of resources on improvisation and a wide range of musical interests.*

Expressive Therapy Concepts • Lynn Miller
http://expressivetherapy.org/
> *A non-profit organization dedicated to bringing the healing power of the arts to our community through expressive arts programs, education, and community arts.*

http://lynnmiller.org/
> *Lynn Miller is a certified Music Therapist, vocalist, guitarist, dancer, and visual artist with a passion for improvisation.*

Group Motion
http://groupmotion.org/
> *A company of performing artists offering workshops to members of the public to explore dance through improvisation.*

Growth in Motion • Franchon Shur
http://growthinmotion.org/
> *This holistic technique connects the body, mind and spirit through movement, body awareness, and creative expression.*

The Inner Game of Music • Barry Green
http://innergameofmusic.com/
> ***What is the Inner Game?*** *The Inner Game, in terms of music, has to do with avoiding those voices of doubt, judgment, and confusion, so that we can listen to and feel the music as we play.*

InterPlay • *Cynthia Winton-Henry*

http://bodywisdom.org/ • http://interplay.org/

InterPlay is a set of practical tools and ideas to help individuals and communities thrive. InterPlay helps us reclaim our lives and get more of what we want, whatever that might be.

Jazzbooks.com • *Jamey Aebersold*

http://jazzbooks.com

Offers a quite extensive selection of jazz education materials.

Kristin Korb

http://kristinkorb.com/

A bassist and singer.

The Listening Book *and* The Musical Life • *W. A. Mathieu*

Books

http://listeningbookaudio.com/index.htm

Audio edition of the author's book presenting exercises designed to help you explore and expand your capacity for listening, appreciate the connection between sound, music, and every-day life and discover the creative possibilities of music-making.

Living Tao Foundation • *Chungliang Al Huang*

http://livingtao.org/

Living Tao Foundation is a non-profit educational and cultural arts foundation. We provide programs in Tai Ji and contemporary Taoist philosophy and related disciplines.

Curt Moore

> http://curtmoore.com/

>> *Curt Moore is co-leader of the five-piece Latin-Jazz group, Soul Sauce. The band draws on the rich body of Afro-Cuban and Brazilian-influenced jazz, as well as incorporating original works and unique arrangements of contemporary, standard, and obscure jazz tunes.*

The Mozart Effect Resource Center • Don Campbell

> http://mozarteffect.com/

>> *Discover the transformational powers of music for health, education, and well-being.*

Music for People • David Darling

> http://musicforpeople.org/

>> *Music for People is dedicated to re-vitalizing your music-making and promoting music as a means of self-expression and offers music improvisation workshops throughout the year, as well as a four-year program called the Musicianship and Leadership Program.*

> daviddarling.com/

>> *A "maverick cellist" whose prolific collection of recordings and innovative performance style represent an eclectic variety of musical genres.*

Music in the Moment • Ron Kravitz

> http://musicinthemoment.com/

>> *Music in the Moment, The Songs within You, and Improvisational Workshops for Everyone focus on discovering and exploring one's own inner world of rhythm and sound.*

Nexus Percussion • Bob Becker
    http://www.nexuspercussion.com/
        *A professional touring percussion ensemble with an
        emphasis on improvisation.*

niadanielle.com • Danielle Woermann
    http://niadanielle.com/
        *Nia is an expressive Body-Mind movement and
        lifestyle practice, embracing fitness and health which
        combines carefully selected movements from yoga,
        tai chi, tae kwon do, jazz, modern dance and other
        movement forms.*

Susan Osborn
    http://susanosborn.com/
        Singer, songwriter, and photographer.

Rhythmic Connections • Mary Knysh
    http://rhythmicconnections.com/
        *The innovative, interactive, inspiring work of Mary
        Knysh inspires everyone to participate in the joyful
        experience of music improvisation. Her fun and
        uplifting musical programs have been widely praised
        for enhancing creativity and self-expression.*

Alan Scofield
    http://alanscofield.com/
        *Choreographer, performance coach, arts educator,
        and founder of Young Imaginations, a nonprofit
        agency offering multicultural music and dance
        classes to approximately 10, 000 children in the San
        Francisco Bay Area each year.*

SpiritGrass • Clint Goss
> http://spiritgrass.com/
>> *SpiritGrass is a unique collaboration between the renowned jazz and bluegrass artist Eric Miller and world instrument troubadour Clint Goss.*

Suzuki Method WWW Network
> http://suzuki-music.com/
>> *Teacher directories and information, information about lessons and study and teacher resources.*

Total Rhythm Fitness Classes • Robert Wallace
> http://totalrhythm.com/
>> *Fitness and drumming classes for children, youth, and adults.*

UCanDanc' African Healing Arts • Masankho Banda
> http://ucandanc.org/
>> *The Mission of UcanDanc' is to build peace, inspire diversity and inclusion and foster healing using InterPlay, dance, music, drums and stories.*

The Vox Mundi Project • Sylvia Nakkach
> http://voxmundiproject.com/
>> *The Vox Mundi Project (Voice of the Worlds) is an international nonprofit organization devoted to teaching and preserving the richness of indigenous musical traditions, combining music, service, and spiritual practice.*

The Walden School Teacher Training Institute • Patricia Plude
> http://waldenschool.org/teacher/faculty.shtml
>> *Director of the Walden School's Teacher Training Institute, which offers professional development opportunities that help music educators more effectively guide the creative voices of their students.*

About the Author

Barry Green served as Principal Bassist of the Cincinnati Symphony for twenty-eight years. As former Executive Director of the International Society of Bassists, he is currently directing a young bassist program for the San Francisco Symphony Education Department, teaches privately, and is the organizer of the Northern California Bass Club.

Former Principal Bassist with the California Symphony and the Sun Valley Idaho Summer Symphony, Green has been performing for young audiences in schools in the Bay Area as well as at workshops and concerts on tour. Green studied with the legendary bassist François Rabbath and wrote *The Popular Bass Method* in collaboration with Bay Area jazz bassist Jeff Neighbor.

Green is author of *The Inner Game of Music* with W. Timothy Gallwey, which deals with musicians reaching their potential in performance and learning and has sold over 250,000 copies worldwide.

Green seminars, workshops, and personal appearances sometimes include a unique lecture/concert called Journey into the Mind and Soul of the Musician that demonstrates concepts described in *The Inner Game of Music* and *The Mastery of Music,* based on interviews with over 120 world-famous musicians on topics of courage, passion, creativity, discipline, humility, and more. It deals with qualities of greatness from the human spirit that transcend all professions.

Additional information about Barry Green, his current activities, calendar of appearances, and more is available at http:// www. innergameofmusic.com/